DEVELOPMENT AND
COMMUNICATION MORPHOSIS

DEVELOPMENT AND
COMMUNICATION MORPHOSIS

DISCARD

Gaurav Sharma

ISBN : 978-93-5128-037-8
Price : ₹ 170

First Published 2014

Published by

Kalpaz Publications
C-30, Satyawati Nagar,
Delhi-110052
Ph. : 9212142040
E-mail: kalpaz@hotmail.com

Laser Typesetting : Sanya Computers, Delhi
Printed at : G. Print Process, Delhi

Cataloging in Publication Data--DK

Courtesy: D.K. Agencies (P) Ltd. <docinfo@dkagencies.com>

Sharma, Gaurav, 1992-
    Development and communication morphosis / Gaurav Sharma.
    p. cm.
    Includes bibliographical references (p.   ).
    ISBN 9789351280378

    1. Communication in economic development--India. 2. Communication--Social aspects--India. 3. Mass media--India. I. Title.

DDC 338.90014   23

Dedication
For YOU, my dearest friend!
and
This book is dedicated to all the earth mates holding a scope of development in their lives.

Contents

Foreword

This morning I had a chance to peruse Gaurav's manuscript.... The book is a commendable and passionate effort (something which I like to encourage, especially with young people). My perception on perusing the volume is that it is written in the format of a "briefing" book — i.e. here are some important things one should know.

However, in its present state, the volume is just that – a briefing book. It is descriptive and selective in what it chooses to focus on (as all books do) and if such is what Gaurav wishes to publish, so be it.

I personally would encourage him to raise the bar for himself and for the students in a *Bachelor of Journalism* programme.... Put in some critical analysis.... Some attention to new and digital media (and what it means for development).... Some case studies.... Put some Umph and chutzpah in it!

However, this is Gaurav's book and not mine, and I want to be helpful to him in a way that he will be more proud of his work, moving forward.

My best wishes to him.

Dr. Arvind Singhal

Professor of Communication and Director
of the Social Justice Initiative
University of Texas, El - Paso, USA

Preface

The concept of development seems to be very simple to most of the people related to the field of development and communication. It is so because they simply tend to overlook or neglect its deeper aspects, as in this fast forward lifestyle, everybody is in a hurry; a hurry to reach somewhere, and yet nowhere. No one wants to be engaged with such complex issues or subjects which require great dedication, determination, supporting thought process, strong analytical approach and confidence in order to be dealt with.

But in reality, the term 'development' has a whole new avenue in itself. During the period of my research and literature review for writing this book, I observed that many prominent authors and scholars often equate development with economic growth only. Though economic growth is the major factor which contributes to the development of a society or country, yet it is not the only factor. In my opinion, the factor which contributes the most in the development of any society or country is the improved thought process initiated towards bringing a change; a change for the betterment which leads to social growth. Society's greater participation, innovative thinking and the zeal to rise above all and come forward inall the fields will take the respective countries towardsan all-around development.

As far as this book is concerned, it is an attempt from my side to simplify the various concepts and paradigms associated with development. The struggle of my fellow classmates and my juniors in college to find books for the Development Communication course outlined for them gave me a boost to write this book. Though there have been stocks of lectures, documents and seminars related to these areas but a book demystifying all important concepts for the young learners and beginners in Development Communication is rare to be found.

This book demystifies the theories, practices, approaches, case studies and analysis related to the field of development communication. It provides the reader with the meaning and acceptance of development communication at both international and national level. Also it will introduce the readers to different and important schemes, initiatives, acts and projects launched by the Government of India in order to bring the country towards development. Efforts have been made to keep this book as simple and suitable as possible for young learners and aspirants related to the field of Development Communication.

All the more this book is based on the latest syllabus recommended by Guru Gobind Singh Indraprastha University, Dwarka, New Delhi for the Bachelor of Journalism and Mass Communication degree programme. Being a communication analyst and a student myself, I have tried my best to make this subject clear to understand and simple to remember for all the students studying development communication not only in GGSIPU, but in all the colleges and Universities across the country at all levels.

The book is an absolute example of literary art. If read with full dedication and interest in order to understand the respective subject, this book will definitely prove its legacy to the readers. It meets its objective of being a textbook as well as a reference book for development communication studies.

With that, I hope this book will surely help you out even when others would fail to do so.

Gaurav Sharma

September 15th, 2013
New Delhi

Acknowledgements

I am highly indebted to my publisher, Kalpaz Publications for showing their interest in publishing my book.

I would like to express my gratitude to Dr. Neeru Johri, (HOD, Department of Communication Studies, Jagannath International Management School, New Delhi) for teaching me this subject during my third semester of the Bachelors Programme in Journalism and Mass Communication.

I am also very thankful to Mr. Hemant Kumar Uppal, (Technical Officer, NIHFW Press, Munirka, New Delhi) who initiated the zeal in me for writing books.

Also, my academic experience in college would not have been this much interesting, full of contentment and learning without the support of my dear teachers. In particular, I thank Dr. Pooja Rana, Dr. Ritu Sood, Dr. Kiran Bala, Ms. Deepa Zutshi, Ms. Sanyogita Choudhary, Ms. Shikha Gupta, Ms. Shikha Kukreja, Ms. Manasvi Maheshwari, Ms. Sakshi Arya and Mr. Anish Saxena.

And as I keep the best for the last, I would now like to thank Dr. Ravi Kumar Dhar (Director, Jagannath International Management School, New Delhi) for always motivating me through the course of my academic and personal life. He is a visionary and a great person who owns an incredible degree of intellect.

1

Understanding Development

The concept of development is really very vast in its context. It is very easy to understand, yet very hard to explain. The meaning of development cannot be caged or constrained into a single definition. In fact, there is no such specific or single definition for the word 'development'.

For an objective understanding, let me give you few definitions of the word 'development' given by some prominent and authentic sources.

The Oxford English Dictionary states the following definitions of the word 'development':

> 'The process of developing or being developed; An event constituting a new stage in a changing situation; The process of converting land to a new purpose by constructing buildings or making use of its resources; The process of starting to be affected by an ailment or feeling; The process of treating photographic film with chemicals to make a visible image.'

The United Nations Development Programme uses a more detailed definition of development. According to them, development is 'to lead long and healthy lives, to be knowledgeable, to have access to the resources needed for a decent standard of living and to be able to participate in the life of a community'.

A manual for news agency reporters brought out by Indian Institute of Mass Communication defines it as: The removal of poverty, the lessening of disparity between regions and classes, the building up of technological infrastructure, modernisation of society through shedding feudalism, tribalism and superstitions, the gradual achievement of economic self-reliance. (Ganesh: 83).

And last but certainly not the least, edited, multilingual, free online encyclopedia viz. Wikipedia itself has too much of data or rather is confused when it comes to providing the meaning of 'development'. It simply states that, development may refer to:

Land Use: Green Development, Land Development, Urban Planning, Transit Oriented Development and so on...

Science and Technology: Artificial Development, Drug Development, Human Development, Child Development, Youth Development, Photographic Development, Web Development, Software Development and so on...

Social Science: Development Studies, Community Development, Economic Development, Rural Development, Sustainable Development and so on...

International and Regional: International Development, Regional Development, Multilateral Development and so on...

Business: Business Development, Career Development, Corporate Development, New Product Development, Leadership Development, Personal Development, Professional

Development and so on...

Now you have to decide first, that which development you are talking about. A little confusing. Isn't it??

So given above were some of the definitions of the word 'development' given by some well-known and trusted sources. It's clear that to define development in a single definition is not possible at all. The meaning of development is different for different people. But these definitions and explanations are a bit contentious and do not constitute a general definition from the communication point of view.

Now take a look at these definitions (social aspect) given by some development scholars:

1. Inayatullah (1967)

'Development is a change towards patterns of society that allows better realisation of human values and also society, to have greater power over its environment, political destiny and enables its individuals to gain better control over themselves.'

—Inayatullah

2. Everett Rogers (1976)

'Development is a participatory process of social change in a society that brings both social and material advancement (including greater equality, freedom and other valued qualities) for majority of people through their pursuit for gaining greater control over environment.'

—Everett Rogers

3. Deepa Zutshi Fotedar[1] (2013)

'Development, as it says, is a vast term that encapsulates various aspects, be it economic—where we discuss the increasing real per capita income of a country over a long period of time; be it the social development–where we discuss upward movement of the entire social system. The process of development not means mere increase in the per capita income or mere industrialization but the overall development of society and its members, where every individual is self-sufficient and self-reliant.'

—Deepa Zutshi

Let me sum up all these and provide you with a simple and general meaning of development.

'Development means a progression from a simpler or lower to a more advanced, mature, or complex form or stage. It can also be defined as the gradual advancement or growth through a series of progressive changes (generally positive). Development is basically the all-round upgradation and upliftment which is attained with the course of time. It is a continuous and an ever evolving process, not one level. It is a path to achieve certain goals and often equated with the degree of improvement and positive changes or modifications'.

---

1. Deepa Zutshi is presently serving as an Assistant Professor in Department of Communication Studies of Jagannath International Management School, New Delhi. She has done her Masters from the prestigious Indian Institute of Modern Management (IIMM), Pune. She is a communication research aspirant and holds a remarkable interest in development communication.

Development is primarily the activation of a country's human and material resources in order to increase the production of goods and services, thereby leading to the general progress and welfare of its people. In the broadest sense development can be defined as an upward directional movement of society from lesser to greater levels of energy, efficiency, quality, productivity, complexity, comprehension, creativity, enjoyment and accomplishment.

The term modernisation, industrialization, globalisation etc. are the contributing factors of the process called development. In any country, development ensures the empowerment of its human resources, natural resources, financial resources and social well-being. Development is about change. It is about changing for the better. It could be about social or economic change for improvement or progress. Every nation, individual or even a microorganism for that matter strives against under-development in order to be in a better condition and to attain development in a continuous manner.

Stages in the Process of Social Development

Development whether social, human, economic, political, infrastructural or cultural, occurs slowly over time. It is the irregular and unconscious process that occurs with zig-zags, with forward motions and set-backs too. Development encompasses a step by step framework which is programmed to achieve the final goal in a steady continuous manner.

There are essentially three stages in the process of social development. They are as follows:

Social Preparedness: This is the very first stage in the social development. In this stage, the society is prepared to move to a higher level of progression/or development through its surplus energies, resources, and awareness of possibilities. Surplus energy and awareness aspires the society to react upon these possibilities to come out in reality. Hence we can say that surplus energy, awareness of possibilities or/ opportunities and aspiration for advancement are the pre requisites that buckle up a society for new development initiatives.

Initiation/ or Role of Pioneering Individuals: The second stage of development is initiation towards achieving that higher level of development governed by the actions and roles of the pioneering individuals of the society. Pioneering individuals are those who come out from the regular and existing trend and try something new, something different. These are the agents who express their want of the society to upgrade to a higher level in action. Through their extraordinary vision and conscious action, these individuals express a few aspects of their aspirations that the society is aware of only partially. A pioneer is a common man with an uncommon or rather extraordinary thinking; he/she breaks the mould, revealing new possibilities yet stands within the social environment and not outside it.

Recognition, Acceptance and Assimilation: This is the third and essentially the last stage of the development process. This stage governs the recognition, acceptance and assimilation of the initiatives of these pioneering individuals. At this stage, the society fully accepts, adopts and organizes these initiatives and possibilities proposed and suggested by the pioneers. Ultimately it progresses towards the development.

Lastly, I consider it essential to provide you with the list of 18 key principles regarding development (social), which will give you a quick overview of the entire concept. These are as follows:

Development is a process not a programme. Development is not the result of a set of policies or programmes. It is the result of a process by which society moves from lesser to greater levels of energy, efficiency, quality, productivity, multiplicity, comprehension, creativity, enjoyment and accomplishment.

The process of development occurs by the creation of higher levels of organizations in societies capable of accomplishing greater acts with more efficient use of social energies. Society develops by organizing and using all the knowledge, human energies and material resources at its disposal to fulfill its aspirations. Organisation is the practical application of knowledge in action. It is the technology or the know-how for social accomplishment.

Political, social, economic and technological development are various expressions and dimensions in the development of the human collective. The same principles of development are applicable to all fields of social existence.

The same principles are applicable for development at the levels of the individuals, the organisations and the society.

A society is prepared for development when it possesses the requisite surplus energy, awareness and aspiration.

Surplus energy is the fuel for development. Each developmental achievement requires an enormous investment of energy in new and higher forms of behaviour. Surplus energy is generated when society has fully organised and mastered activities at its current level of development. The development and application of mind energizes the society by technological and organisational innovation, spread of education, acceptance of new ideas and higher values.

Energy is released when the society becomes aware of new opportunities and has the collective will to exploit the opportunities. The driving force for development is the progressive growth of the social collectives' knowledge and awareness of opportunities and the social aspiration or will for higher accomplishment.

The social organisation consists of a single interconnected fabric. The threads and the weave of the fabric are formed by the multidimensional interaction of social activities, organisations, institutions and values. This fabric varies in thickness and density of weave, being most concentrated in large, highly developed urban centers. Development is the process by which the fabric of the social organisation increases in density, quality, complexity, and geographic extension.

Society develops through the three overlapping stages—physical, vital, and mental. Each stage is characterised by the predominance of one of the three attributes of human consciousness. The progression from one stage to the next stimulates an exponential increase in the productivity and accomplishments of the society.

The natural process of development is unconscious. It proceeds by a slow, cumbersome, trial and error process from experience to knowledge. Conscious development moves in the other direction from knowledge to experience. The more conscious the process, the more rapid the progress. Education is an essential prerequisite for conscious development.

The society gives formed creative expression to its collective subconscious urge for development through the initiative of pioneering individuals.

The response of society to the initiative of the pioneer depends on its prior preparedness. Initiatives that are too far beyond the society's preparedness are opposed, rejected or ignored. These pioneers are considered rebels. Those that embody the next step in the collective march are embraced, often after initial resistance, they are imitated and eventually accepted by the collective. These pioneers are accepted as leaders.

Once a new activity is accepted, society establishes new organisations, policies and laws to support it. When social acceptance of the activity becomes complete, the activity matures into an institution that no longer requires the support of specialised organisations, policies and laws to promote it. At a further stage the activity is transmitted to the future generations through the families and becomes a part of the culture of the society.

When society seeks to move to the next, higher stage of development, existing beliefs, attitudes, behaviours and forms of organisations become obstacles that have to be overcome in order for the transition to take place. Progression towards each further stage involves a change in attitude and lifestyle.

The speed of social development increases as awareness of opportunities spreads, aspirations increases, conscious knowledge of organisation grows, attitudes become more progressive, and infrastructure is put in place.

Development takes place on the foundation of four types of infrastructure–physical, social, mental and psychological. Only the first of these is subject to any inherent limits. As development progresses, it relies more and more on non-material resources.

Resources also are of four types–physical, social, mental and psychological.

Mind is the creator of all resources. The application of human intelligence and inventiveness converts a substance into a resource. Increasing knowledge, increases the productivity of its resources, even physical resources. Therefore, mind is the ultimate resource that gives value to all the others.

2

Understanding Development Communication

After you understood what development actually is all about, understanding development communication would be easier for you. When we refer to development communication, it is about such communication that can be used for development. As the name itself suggests, development communication governs the usage of communication for development. It is about using communication to change or improve something.

Development communication is also referred to as communication for development, development support communication and more recently as communication for social change. Out of all these terms, "development communication" is the most relevant. The main reason for adopting the term "development communication" has been that of keeping the original two terms delineating the fields' scope (that is, "communication" and "development") while addressing some of the shortcomings of other similar terms. The term "development support communication" has been criticized for considering communication as an add=on component used only to support other projects' components, while the term "communication for development" reinforces the wrong idea that any kind of communication used in the developmental context (for example, corporate communication) shares the same theoretical and methodological features.

The term "development communication" was first introduced in the early 1970s by Dr. Nora Cruz Quebral. She is a prominent personality in the field of development communication. Recently, Dr. Quebral, professor Emeritus, received the 2013 UPAA Lifetime Distinguished Achievement Award from the University of the Philippines Alumni Association (UPAA) during the UP General Alumni-Faculty Homecoming and Reunion held at the Bahayng Alumni in UP, Diliman campus on June 22, 2013.

According to her 'Development Communication is the art and science of human communication linked to a society's planned transformation from a state of poverty to one that of dynamic socio-economic growth that makes for greater equity and the larger unfolding of individual potential.' It is observed that development communication is a purposeful communication effort geared towards realisation of human potentials and transformation from a bad situation to a good one.

According to the World Bank, Development Communication is the integration of strategic communication in development projects.

Gary Coldevin notes that development communication mobilises people to participate in developmental activities. He defines development communication as 'the systematic utilisation of appropriate communication channels and techniques to increase people's participation in development and to inform, motivate, and train rural populations, mainly at the grassroots level.'

Dr. Andrew A. Moemeka states his views on development communication in Africa Media Review, Vol. 3 No. 3, 1989. There it is mentioned that development communication is the application of the processes of communication to the development process. It is the use of the principles and practices of exchange of ideas to development objectives.

Development Communication Division of the World Bank (DevComm) considers development communication as an interdisciplinary field based on empirical research that helps to build consensus while it facilitates the sharing of knowledge to achieve positive change in development initi tives. It is not only about effective dissemination of information but also about using empirical research and a two-way communication among stakeholders.

The other definition emerged at the First World Congress of Communication for Development, held in Rome in October 2006. It is included in the document known as the Rome Consensus, in which more than 900 participants of the Congress (World Bank et al. 2007: xxxiii) agreed to conceive it as a social process based on dialog using a broad range of tools and methods. It is also about seeking change at different levels, including listening, building trust, sharing knowledge and skills, building policies, debating, and learning for sustained and meaningful change. It is not public relations or corporate communication.

Communication for development is not restricted to the channels of mass media only. It also uses all other effective means of communication viz. interpersonal, face-to-face, small group, the stage play, a picture, or even a billboard.

Development communication encompasses all those communication strategies, practices, initiatives and plans which are drafted and hence implemented in order to change, improve or develop something (socially). Objective of development communication is to inform, educate, persuade and mobilise the people of a community towards a progressive and better state and condition. Communication for development has to do with the use of communication methods, forms and channels in the process of development. Its purpose is to bring about social change and betterment through people's participation.

Development communication is the blend of applicable communication skills and development practices. It is primarily oriented towards the human aspects of development. Development communication is concerned with rural, urban and suburban problems.

The main purpose of development communication is to support sustainable change in development operations by engaging key stakeholders. It establishes a conducive environment to assess risks and opportunities; disseminate information; induce behaviour and social change.

The science which uses communication to change and motivate people through education and inspiration towards development is called development communication.

Development communication brings about a planned growth intended to promote human development, reducing, if not eradicating poverty, unemployment and other social inequalities. It is engaged not only in mere reporting of facts or opinions, but also in teaching the people and leading them towards action. It imparts and shares ideas to nurture and cultivate the proper attitudes, skills and values that are needed to develop. In short, development communication is a communication science that assists in developmental goals.

Development Communicator: There is no such profession whose members are known as Development Communicators. Any communication practitioner who helps people with a disadvantage to better their lives so that they can realise their potential, is a development communicator. A development communicator acts like a bridging agent who fills the gap between the sources (experts, scientists and bureaucrats) and the receivers (at grass root level). A development communicator should have the ability to recognise and understand micro level needs of the people. He should be socially, culturally, and environmentally sensitive and efficient in communication relationships.

3

Understanding Paradigm

The last few decades witnessed a proliferation in the use of the word "paradigm", in connection with many subjects. But the question still remains unnoticed: What exactly is paradigm? And where did it come from? When I studied development communication, I observed that most of my fellow classmates were not familiar with the word "Paradigm". When asked by the teacher, about the meaning of the word, they used to make ugly faces and would often provide a shallow definition. Before studying further about the theories and paradigms of development, I consider it necessary to provide you with the meaning and definition of the word "paradigm" in context of development communication.

In simple words, paradigm means school of thoughts. It encompasses distinct concepts or thought patterns about any subject or field.

It is a certain way of thinking and developing a thought process about something which is generally acceptable in the society. Paradigm is the set of ideas that are used for understanding or explaining something, especially in a particular subject. It is a framework containing the basic assumptions, perceptions, ways of thinking and methodology over a specific subject or topic which is accepted by the society or members of the community.

The way in which most of the people of the society think, understand, perceive, believe and hence constitute a common conscience over a specific subject, topic, field or area sets the paradigm of that very subject or field. Let us study each of them in detail.

The Dominant Paradigm: Modernisation

This was the very first paradigm of development which dates back to the period soon after the World War II and has been called the dominant paradigm because of its pervasive impact on most aspects of development. The western model for development predominated in the 1950s and 1960s. Rogers (1960) called this the "dominant paradigm" of development as it exercised a dominant influence in the field of development. The emphasis of this model was that development could be achieved by increased productivity, economic growth and industrialisation, through heavy industries, capital intensive technologies, urbanization, centralized planning. Development was measured by gross national product (GNP), total or per capita income. There was a shift from a static, agricultural, primitive and rigid society to a dynamic, industrialised, urbanised and socially mobile nation.

Daniel Lerner and Wilbur Schramm (1964) supported the dominant paradigm and advocated automation and technology for development and change of a society. They made significant contributions in identifying the role of communication, for technological development.The main and central concept of this paradigm was to solve development problems by "modernising" underdeveloped and developing countries. This paradigm suggested to the underdeveloped countries as to how to be effective in following the footsteps of richer, more developed countries.

After World War II a number of countries became independent; several years of colonial domination had left them underdeveloped and economically poor. Thus development was equated with economic growth at that time. The countries having more economic resources were considered as more developed than those having less economic resources.

Also, communication was equated with the dissemination of messages and information aimed at moderniaing "backward" countries and their people. Due to the overestimated belief that mass media is an extremely powerful and effective tool for persuading audiences to change their attitudes and behaviours, mass media was at the center of the communication initiatives taken at that time. These initiatives and campaigns relied heavily on the traditional model of communication i.e. the vertical one way model which is Sender - Message - Channel - Receiver (SMCR). Thus, in the dominant paradigm the communication flow was one way which was top-down vertical communication from the authorities to the people, the mass media channels were used to mobilize the people for development and the audience was assigned a passive role of acceptance of the social change.

The Opposing Paradigm: Dependency

In the 1960s the modernization paradigm was opposed strongly, which in turn resulted in the emergence of an alternative theoretical model rooted in a political and economic perspective: the dependency theory. The proponents of this school of thoughts criticised some of the core assumptions of the dominant paradigm.

The dominant paradigm put the responsibility, and the blame, for the causes of underdevelopment exclusively on the recipients. The other factors responsible for the underdevelopment such as external, social, historical and natural factors were neglected under the paradigm and emergence of the dependency paradigm was the blame on dominant paradigm of being very western-centric, refusing or neglecting any alternative path to development.

In the field of communication, the dependency theorists emphasised the importance of the link between communication and culture but still the basic conception remained rooted in the linear, one way model. One of the thorny issues was the demand for a more balanced and equitable exchange of communication, information, and cultural programmes among the rich and poor countries. Although the dependency theory had gained a significant impact in the 1970s, in the 1980s it started to lose relevance gradually in tandem with the failure of the alternative economic models proposed by its proponents.

The Emerging Paradigm: Participation

When modernization paradigm failed to keep up its promises and its methods came increasingly under fire, dependency theorists failed to provide any alternative method and a successful alternative model, a different approach focusing on people's participation began to emerge. This approach was named as the emerging paradigm i.e. participation of the people.

This paradigm stressed the importance of cultural realties of development and was less oriented to the political-economic dimension. Under this paradigm the development focus had shifted from mere economic growth to include other social dimensions needed to ensure meaningful results in the long run for attaining development. Sustainability and people's participation became key elements of this new paradigm, as acknowledged by the consensus built by the definition of Millennium Development Goals and the World Bank (1994: 3): 'Internationally, emphasis is being placed on the challenge of sustainable development, and participation is increasingly recognised as a necessary part of sustainable development strategies.'

This new paradigm is also changing the way communication is conceived and applied. It shifts the emphasis from information dissemination to situation analysis, from mere persuasion to participation. Communication models are being designed horizontally, i.e. bi-directional rather than vertical, uni=directional as they were in earlier paradigms. Emphasis is given on sender as well as receiver in order to promote people's participation in development initiatives.

4

Theories of Development

The definition of development is different for different countries, depending upon their resources viz. human resources, financial resources, natural resources and economic resources. For some countries development may be attaining optimum literacy rate, while for some it may be attaining infrastructural advancement or natural afforestation.

After the Second World War, a number of countries became free and independent. As they were earlier being ruled by other colonial entities (colonial rule) they became underdeveloped and hence, attaining development became their first and foremost priority. As a result, a number of theories and alternatives emerged out in order to eliminate underdevelopment, these theories were nothing but, analysed concepts and trials proposed or/suggested by some of the greatest economists and visionaries so as to attain development.

Let us study each of them in detail.

All these theories and approaches are broadly classified into two groups i.e. **Unilinear** world view of development and **Non-unilinear** world view of development.

Now, **Unilinear** world view of development simply suggests that, if underdeveloped countries want to develop, then they have to follow the footprints of the developed nations. Unilinear means moving from one step to another logically and in a systematic way to attain development. The western developed countries followed and practiced some specific kinds of processes, and they have achieved a kind of better standard of living. These countries are setting up an example for other countries when it comes to development. Even the people living in the western developed countries are enjoying certain consumer items, services and facilities which are not easily available for the people living in other parts of the world and that too at an affordable cost. Due to their remarkable influence across the globe and in the international scene, these western countries have become the principle model of development for the developing or underdeveloped nations.

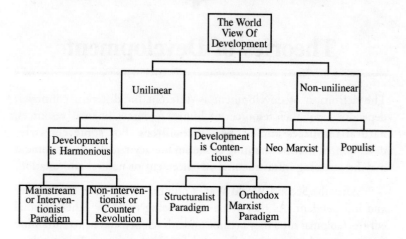

Unilinear world view of development therefore proposes that development means to become more like the western countries. If underdeveloped or developing countries will follow the same path, as that of the developed countries they will surely achieve their developmental goals and attain high standard of living. Developed countries redefine the benchmarks of development and hence the other countries should follow their footprints. For becoming like the west certain institutional and economical hurdles such as monarchy, closed economy system, dictatorship etc. must be removed in order to initialise developmental processes in the underdeveloped or developing countries.

On the other hand the **Non-unilinear** world view of development suggests that development does not mean becoming like the western countries. Western countries have their own historical background, natural and financial resource based conditions which are different than that of the underdeveloped nations. It may not be possible for the developing countries to reach that position as that of the developed countries. The underdeveloped countries should not follow the footprints of the western countries and hence, should find other alternative ways in order to become developed countries.

Types of Unilinear Theories

Theories falling under Unilinear world view are further classified into two categories: **Harmonious Development** and **Contentious Development**.

Harmonious Development: These theories suggest that development is a harmonious process. This means that developmental process benefits all the rich as well as the poor people, and rich as well as poor countries. If a developmental plan is executed, both rich and poor people will be equally affected and benefited by it.

Contentious Development: These theories consider development primarily as a conflicting process. It encompasses that rich countries and rich people are exploiting the poor countries and poor people respectively. Contentious theory simply refers that development is a contradictory process where the poor is exploited by the rich. The rich countries and rich people get all the benefits and the poor countries and poor people remain deprived of being benefited by the fruits of development.

Now, theories which suggest development as a harmonious process have two sub categories, *Mainstream or Interventionist Paradigm and Non-interventionist or Counter-revolution Paradigm* respectively.

Mainstream or Interventionist Paradigm suggests that active role and intervention of the government or the state authority is an essential requirement for the development to happen. According to these theories, the countries having an active government intervention develop easily and rapidly. While on the contrary, the **Counter-revolution/Non-intervention** theories emphasise on non-intervention by the state or non-involvement of the government and advocate the efficiency and importance of the market in promoting development.

These theories propose that government intervention and involvement is not essentially required in order to be developed. But, markets (the forces that determine demand, supply, cost, pricing and production of goods, services and commodities) should be given priority as they boost the economic development which will ultimately lead to an overall development of that very country.

The theories which suggest that development is a contentious and conflicting process further have two sub categories viz. *Structuralist Paradigm and Orthodox Marxist Paradigm.*

Structuralist Paradigm refers that the underdevelopment in countries is a result of the internal as well as international system and structure of production of goods, services and commodities.

Internally, the developing nations are essentially dependent on the production and export of primary products like oil, tea, rubber, sugar, Iron and other minerals and raw materials. While on an international platform, the developed countries (capitalist west) produce and export 'manufactured' and 'processed' goods.

Factors like low level of industrialisation, obsolete technology and less demand leads to the exploitation of the underdeveloped countries by the developed countries as these developed countries sell their manufactured goods at high price and buy raw materials from developing countries at low cost. Therefore, these theories suggest that if less developed countries want development, they are required to change the system or structure of production increasingly, in favor of manufactured goods through capital based technology and industrialisation. After doing this, underdeveloped countries can also develop like the west.

On the other hand the **Orthodox Marxist Paradigm** considers that conflict and contradictions in the development of capitalism are inevitable. It is almost impossible to completely avoid these conflicts and contradictions in the development of capitalism. These conflicts can only be eliminated and resolved through revolution, which will then usher in the next phase of development.

Types of Non-Unilinear Theories

Theories falling under Non-unilinear world view of development are further classified into two main categories, *Neo-Marxist* and *Populist* view.

Neo-Marxist paradigm means the expansion of traditional Marxist thoughts. This concept is aimed towards incorporating principles of Marxism thought into modern political and economic systems. This view stresses the inter-connectedness of development and underdevelopment, of traditional and modern, and indeed many other social, political and economic factors. The main aim of development of the Neo-Marxism theory was to cater to the several political and social problems which traditional Marxist thought was unable to answer. The Neo-Marxist approach to development of economics is connected with dependency of countries-and-world systems-theories.

Economists like Paul Baran and A.G Frank may be called as Neo-Marxists. According to Baran, underdevelopment of most of the world was a direct result of the dynamics of monopoly and capitalism, which had blocked the primary accumulation of capital in the underdeveloped regions, and smothered their novice industries.

Neo-Marxism describes a loose movement of political and social theorists who interpreted Marxism with an emphasis on the humanism and idealism concepts of Karl Marx's early works. Contrary to the orthodox (or traditional) Marxists, Neo-Marxists sought to explain why political revolution did not take place as Marx predicted and thus explored the phenomena of psychological coercion and liberation.

Populist paradigm, on the other hand questions either the need or the possibility of less developed countries developing on the lines of the already developed capitalist countries. The Gandhian thinking about the appropriate development for countries like India can be considered as a Populist view. Some contribution from E.F Schumacher, who wrote the book 'Small Is Beautiful' can be considered as a part of the Populist view. Theories under this paradigm propose that western type of development has nothing much to commend about in societies like India.

Gandhi thought that the western industrialization had brought along with it immorality, crime and cultural degeneration. Gandhi stressed on making villages as the center of all economic activities. He proposed that development in a country like India (which is agrarian based) should provide employment and livelihood through a network of cottage and village industries.

According to Schumacher, the two severe problems of the less developed countries are mass unemployment and mass migration to the urban areas. This creates a huge gapin the economic accumulation and distribution of that very country. As a result of which the emergence of "dual economics" tends to happen in rural and urban areas of that country, which ultimately separate them from each other, living as two different worlds (one rich, one poor) inside one country.

5

Economic and Social Indicators of Development

Development is a multilayered process that consist of many economic and social factors which determine its degree. A country rich in some of these factors does not necessarily become a developed country. These factors and indicators are just a statistical approach to measure the well-being of a country. There is always a scope of improvement for development in the economy, social environment, standard of living, life expectancy, life span and literacy rate of any country, no matter how highly it is developed.

Let's go through these indicators:

Human Development Index (HDI): HDI is a composite statistic, used to rank countries by their level of 'human development'. HDI of a country primarily governs the standard of living and/or quality of life of the people living in that country. It distinguishes all the countries of the world into four broad categories viz., countries having very high human development, countries having high human development, countries having medium human development and countries with low human development.

HDI was devised and launched by Mahbub-ul-Haq, a Pakistani economist followed by the Indian economist Amartya Sen in the year 1990. It is a comparative measure of degree of literacy, education, life expectancy, standards of living and/or quality of life of the people in a country. HDI is a standard means of measuring the all-round development and well-being of a country. It is widely used in determining the status of a country, i.e., whether that country is developed, developing or underdeveloped. Apart from rating countries on the grounds of development, HDI is also used in measuring the impact of economic policies on the quality of life. States, cities and villages can also have their own HDI depending upon their interest for the same. HDI formula results is a number from 0 to 1, where 1 is considered as the best possible outcome.

Physical Quality of Life Index (PQLI): PQLI is another criterion for determining the quality of life or well-being of a country. The value is the average of three statistics: basic literacy rate, infant mortality rate and life expectancy at age one, all equally weighed on a scale of 0 to 100 scale or mark.

When compared to HDI, PQLI is considered as a less efficient formula for determining the development of a country due to its contradicting and overlapping two factors viz. infant mortality and life expectancy at age one. Apart from this one contradiction, it is also a complex formula and it is very difficult to find the most accurate average of these three statistics as these are qualitative factors and cannot be measured in a quantitative way.

PQLI was Developed for the Overseas

Development Council in the mid 1970s by David Morris as one of the numbers of measurement created due to dissatisfaction with the use of GNP (Gross National Product) as an indicator of development.

Formula for calculating PQLI:

1. Find the percentage of the population that is literate (literacy rate).

2. Find the infant mortality rate (out of 1000 births).

   (B.1) Indexed infant mortality rate = $(166 - B) \times 0.625$

   (C) Find the life expectancy.

   (C.1) Indexed life expectancy = $(C - 42) \times 2.7$

Now find PQLI by $(A + B.1 + C.1) / 3$.

Happy Planet Index (HPI)/Happiness Index: HPI is an index of human well-being and environmental impact. It is the leading global measure of sustainable well-being. It was introduced in the year 2006 by the New Economics Foundation (NEF).

The HPI measures what matters: the extent to which countries deliver long, happy, sustainable lives for the people that live in them. The index uses global data on life expectancy, experienced well-being and ecological[2] footprints to calculate this. HPI is an efficiency measure which ranks countries on the basis of how many long and happy lives they produce per unit of environmental input.

HPI = (Experienced well-being × Life expectancy)/Ecological footprint

Most measures of national progress are actually just measures of economic activity, that is how much we are producing or consuming. By only using indicators like Gross Domestic Product (GDP) to measure success we are not accounting for what really matters, producing happy lives for people at present and in the future.

HPI frames the development of each country in the context of real environmental limits. In doing so it tells us what we instinctively know to be true—that progress is not just about wealth. HPI is measured on a scale of 0 to 100. It is a clear and meaningful barometer of how well a nation is doing. It measures a lot but does not measure everything. Countries that do well on the HPI may suffer from many other problems which are out of the HPI criteria. This is because there is no 100% development and absolute happiness in any country of the world. There is always a scope of improvement and development, no matter how highly developed a country is.

Alongside of the latest report NEF is launching a Happy Planet Charter very soon to facilitate the indexing process and to make it more credible and statistically accurate.

Gross Domestic Product (GDP): GDP is the total market value of all goods and services produced within the country's borders over a

---

2. Ecological footprint is a per capita measure of the amount of land required to sustain a country's consumption patterns; measured in terms of global hectares (g ha) which represent a hectare of land with average productive bio-capacity.

specific period of time, generally one year. It is based on the geographical location of the production. GDP falls under the macroeconomics branch of economics as it deals with the performance, structure, behavior, and decision=making of an economy as a whole, rather than as individual markets. This includes national, regional, and global economies. GDP was first developed by the economist Simon Kuznets.

Measuring GDP is a very complex method, but at its most basic, the calculation can be done in one of the three ways viz., production approach, income approach and expenditure approach. All these three approaches shall approximately give the same results.

In the product approach, the market value of all the finished goods and services is calculated for a period of one year. In the income approach, the sum total of the income of the people living in that particular country is taken into account for one year. Whereas in the expenditure approach, all the expenditure incurred by individuals during the period of one year is taken into account. Ideally all these methods shall provide the same results as they are interconnected to each other.

The expenditure approach works on the principle that all of the products must be bought by somebody, therefore the value of the total product must be equal to people's total expenditures in buying things. The income approach works on the principle that the incomes of the productive factors or producers must be equal to the value of their product, and calculates the GDP by summing up all the incomes of the producers.

However, there are certain limitations of GDP and therefore its use to determine the development of a country has been criticized by many prominent economists around the world. Simon Kuznets stated, 'Distinctions must be kept in mind between quantity and quality of growth, between costs and returns, and between the short and long run goals for more growth should specify more growth of what and for what'.

Another economist, Frank Shostak from an Austrian school argued that GDP is an empty abstraction devoid of any link to the real world, and, therefore, has little or no value in economic analysis. The GDP framework cannot tell us whether final goods and services that were produced during a particular period of time are a reflection of the real wealth expansion, or a reflection of capital consumption. For instance, if a government embarks on the building of a pyramid, which adds absolutely nothing to the well-being of individuals, the GDP framework will regard this as economic growth. In reality, however, the building of the pyramid will divert real funding from wealth=generating activities, thereby stifling the production of wealth.

Apart from these economists, many environmentalists argue that GDP is a poor measure of determining development and social progress because it does not take into account the harm to the environment.

Even after so much of criticism, GDP is one of the main indicators used to measure the economic strength of a country. When GDP is positive, there is a decline in the unemployment and growth in the economy as businesses demand more labor which increases the wages. A bad economy usually means lower profits for companies, which in turn means lower stock prices. Investors really worry about negative GDP growth, which is one of the factors economists use to determine whether an economy is in a recession. Therefore we can say that GDP has a large and notable impact on nearly everyone within the respective economy. That is why it is considered as a major economic indicator of development.

Gross National Product (GNP): GNP is the official market value of all the products and services which are produced by the country's citizens or residents regardless of their location (they may be inside the geographical borders of the country, outside the borders or both). For a simple understanding, let me give you a formula for calculating GNP.

GNP = GDP + any income earned by citizens or residents
from overseas investment-income earned within
the domestic economy by overseas residents.

While GNP measures the output generated by a country's enterprises (whether physically located within the country or abroad) GDP measures the total output produced within a country's borders—whether produced by that country's own local firms or by foreign firms.

The general purpose of using measures such as GNP or GDP is to collect and analyse information related to a country's economic transactions. GNP or GDP provides analysts with an indication of how quickly the business sector of the economy is growing in a country. Therefore GNP is considered as a major economic indicator of development in a country.

Communication: It is the most important social factor and indicator of development for any country or individual. The role of communication in the socio-economic and cultural development at national and international levels has been recognised over the past two decades. The key role of communication in development is to help people change their behaviour. Communication is not only the transmission of messages from sender to receiver through a channel backed up by feedback; but it is a process in which an individuality (community or nation) enters a mental co-operation with another individuality (community or nation) until they constitute a common conscience.

Communication therefore, is the foundation of any progressive change in the individual, society or country. Without proper communication, development is absolutely unthinkable. Communication mobilises the ideas, thoughts and hence the actions between two individuals, communities or countries. It helps in socialising which ultimately leads to the sharing of ideas, policies, innovations, business strategies, economy, health plans and education between two entities. Communication brings the feeling of co-operation and commonality between the entities indulging in it.

Most of the revolutions (industrial revolution and green revolution) around the world or let's say in our country, India are the result of strong communication practices. Every sector whether agricultural, economic, sports, health, education or scientific needs to communicate in order to facilitate their working and proper functioning.

For example, in a country like India, agriculture is the main source of income for more than 60 per cent of the total population as it is the primary activity in which people are engaged. It is only due to good relations and communication strategies between our farmers, between scientists with other farmers between scientists in other countries, that new equipment and techniques are being used in our country as well. As a result of this sharing of technologies, the overall cost of production has decreased and at the same time the productivity has increased. This increases our economic health and thus, pushes us and our country towards development.

Same is the case with all other sectors. With the advent of new technologies and communication practices, all these sectors are improving and are being benefited and in some way or the other are contributing a lot towards development. Therefore, we can say that communication plays the most important role in everybody's life. This is the reason why it is considered as a major social indicator of development.

Democracy: Democracy is a system of government by the whole population or all the eligible members of a state, typically through elected representatives. Democracy, which derives from the Greek word *demos*, or people, is defined, basically, as a government in which the supreme power is vested in the people. It is a polity in which collective decisions (be it laws, policies, procedures) are all the expressions, whether direct or indirect, preferences and choices are collectively the decisions of the citizens in equality of the polity. Democracy thus pertains to the self-rule of a politically constituted social group be it a state or provincial authority, or a city or town. An efficient and corruption free democracy is the base of development in a country.

In some forms, democracy can be exercised directly by the people; in large societies, it is done by the people through their elected agents or representatives. Or, in the memorable phrase of President Abraham Lincoln, democracy is government of the people, by the people, and for the people.

Countries can promote human development for all only when they have governance systems that are fully accountable to the people and when people can participate in its debates and decisions affecting their lives.

6

Millennium Development Goals

Millennium Development Goals (MDGs) are eight internationally accepted development goals or objectives which were officially drafted in the year 2000 at the United Nations headquarters in New York City. The MDGs and targets come from the Millennium Declaration, signed by 189 countries, including 147 heads of state and government, in September 2000.

The UN Millennium Project explains MDGs in detail: "At the Millennium Summit in September 2000 the largest gathering of world leaders in history adopted the UN Millennium Declaration, committing their nations to a new global partnership to reduce extreme poverty and setting out a series of time-bound targets, with a deadline of 2015, that have become known as the Millennium Development Goals.

The Millennium Development Goals (MDGs) are the world's time-bound and quantified targets for addressing extreme poverty in its many dimensions—income poverty, hunger, diseases, lack of adequate shelter, and exclusion—while also promoting gender equality, education, and environmental sustainability. They are also basic human rights—the rights of each person on the planet towards health, education, shelter and security."

These eight goals are listed as follows:

1. Eradicate extreme poverty and hunger

2. Achieve universal primary education

3. Promote gender equality and empower women

4. Reduce child mortality

5. Improve maternal health

6. Combat HIV/AIDS, malaria and other diseases

7. Ensure environmental sustainability

8. Develop a global partnership for development

These MDGs also drive international development code and policy by spelling out the duties and responsibilities of the rich and developed countries to support poor countries through aid, debt relief and market access.

Now let me introduce you with the darker side of the relationship between India and MDGs. According to the recent studies and researched reports, India unfortunately will not be able to achieve crucial MDG targets by the given deadline i.e., year 2015.

According to the 2013 Social Watch India National Report, India's progress towards achieving the MDGs as reported in the latest official MDG Report, is that India is likely to fall short from in a majority of the targets and indicators with respect to Goal 1: poverty and hunger; Goal 3: gender equality; Goal 4: infant mortality, Goal 5: maternal mortality and Goal 7: environmental sustainability; all of which, with the possible exception of environmental sustainability, is appalling. Even the partial successes achieved on targets and indicators with respect to Goal 2: education; Goal 6: health, have a few caveats. For example, the school enrolment rates are ahead of the targets, but the dropout rates are also high, making the enrolment rates meaningless. The incidence of HIV/AIDS has come down, but what is alarming is that HIV/AIDS incidence is increasing in states where it was hitherto low. There are also wide variations in the penetration of information and communication devices as agreed under Goal 8: development partnership. And, as the report indicates; the performance of a majority of states on many of the goals and targets are even more appalling. The quality of achievements that have been made is also far from satisfactory.

Another report published in the online portal of one of the prestigious national newspaper of India 'The Hindu' by Professor K.S. Jacob from Christian Medical College, Vellore, states that India's vast population, its diversity, the variability of services and the differing baselines across regions complicate the achievement of the MDGs.

According to a report of the Press Trust of India (PTI), India's poverty ratio is likely to be 26.7 per cent by 2015 while child mortality ratio is seen to be at 52 per thousand live births, missing the Millennium Development Goals in this regard; according to a government report. According to the Statistical Year Book 2013 released by the Minister of Statistics and Programme Implementation Srikant Kumar Jena, the poverty ratio is likely to be 26.7 per cent compared to the MDG target of 23.9 per cent by 2015. It was 29.8 per cent in 2009-10.

As per MDG, India was required to halve the percentage of population below the national poverty line by 2015 over the 1990 level. In 1990, poverty ratio was 47.8 per cent which came down to 37.2 per cent in 2004-05. India was also required to reduce the child mortality rate to 42 per thousand live births by 2015. However, the current estimates suggest that it would be around 52 by the end of the MDG deadline.

The year book further indicates that India will also miss the infant mortality rate target of 27 per thousand live births by 2015. India is likely to reduce the IMR to 43 per thousand by 2015 from 44 in 2011. As per another MDG target, India is expected to reduce the maternal mortality ratio (MMR) by three quarters, between 1990 and 2015 to 109 per one lakh births. The latest data suggests that MMR would come down to 139 per one lakh births by 2015 from 437 in 1990.

Though India is progressing towards achieving these targets yet it is quite clear from the above facts and statistical data that our country India may fail to meet these goals and objectives by the year 2015, which unfortunately is a bad news for us.

7

Basic Needs Model by Bariloche Foundation

One of the remarkable models in the field of development was the Basic Needs Model (BNM) which was first developed by the Bariloche Foundation in year 1972. The foundation is situated in Argentina. BNM was an attempt to deal directly with world poverty by meeting the basic needs of the lowest 40 per cent income groups in the fields of food, nutrition, health, education, housing through employment and income (Narula Uma, 1994).

BNM approach is not a development strategy by itself, but it is an essential ingredient of patterns or growth underlying the development strategy. The lack of participation of the large sections of the country's population in social, cultural, political and economic activities necessitated the need for the BNM.

BNM was drafted on the concept that the depressed and differently abled groups have the right to enjoy the products and services of the society, be it goods, cultural values or any other fruits of modernization. The dominant and superior group must co=operate in order to bring the possible change through gradual extension and expansion of these products.

At later stages, BNM was intended to include non-material human needs like—to give quality and standard of life to the poor, once the material needs were fulfilled. For achieving normative needs, both mass media and interpersonal channels of communication should be used. However, the third-world countries as a majority rejected the concept of basic needs, though this concept it had originated in the third world itself and it concerned the development of the third world.

Even after the recognition of the BNM at an international level, the developed countries reflected their desire to keep the third world countries as non-competitive, largely pastoral societies, though a little better fed, housed and educated. To sum up, irrespective of these constraints, the basic needs approach has added to the conceptual and operational tools of development.

8

Approaches to Development Communication

Development communication is a multi-layered, multi-dimensional science of communication that assists development goals. To handle development communication in an efficient way, there are varied approaches for it. These are as follows:

Diffusion of Innovation Approach: This approach or concept is based on the central idea that technological and social innovation should be adopted through the diffusion of new ideas, services and products. This approach suggests that the need assessment of the community and the need fulfilment of the community should be done in a better way through innovations and new ideas. Diffusion of both material innovations (economic and technological innovations) and social innovations (social needs and structure) is essential for development.

Based on the needs of the adopters, it is eventually decided whether to accept or reject the innovations. Once the innovation or idea is accepted and well organised by the society, it further expands and tends to reach to every individual of the community, ultimately leading towards development.

Magic Multiplier Approach: Wilbur Schramm was a pioneer in the field of development communication. He proposed a theory that information is a vital element in moving a nation towards development. He called his theory the magic multiplier theory. Though Schramm died in 1987 at the ripe old age of 79, yet his theory is proving its legacy in many Third World countries. The central idea of this approach is that, the mass media plays a magical role in multiplying the effect and impact of the messages and information communicated through them to the target audience.

Mass media is a powerful tool for educating, persuading and mobilising people. Marshall McLuhan, an international authority on mass media and communication also supports Schramm's theory. No matter what the contents of the programmes, he argued that the audiences will watch television, and it commands their attention as no other medium ever has. Mass communications are neither good nor bad, but are rather mystical devices that possess powers to change the way humans lead their lives.

Magic Multiplier approach totally fits the bill when it comes to India's communication revolution. With the advent of mass communication channels and mass media in India, the way of lives of people have shifted entirely to an upper strata. Mass media influences each and every individual to the core. Thus, it would not be wrong to call it a magic multiplier as it wonderfully amplifies the impact of the message which is communicated through it.

Localised Approach: This approach to development communication is also very media oriented. It essentially lays emphasis on interaction with the people by establishing media channels to provide access for the people. Localises approach somehow governs the importance of interpersonal communication too. Initially the problems of the people are identified through personal calls, meetings and discussions by media personnel who are required to enter into a socio-cultural space and contexts of the people. This approach calls for the establishment of local radio, local newspaper or press, local television production or viewing centres as there is a need to cater to specific issues and problems related to the respective society or community.

Through local media, the rural population can talk to themselves, talk to the authorities and participate fully in the construction and dissemination of development messages meant for them. This develops interaction between people and between the pioneers of the society, which in turn, speeds up the development process.

9

Development Support Communication

Erskine Childers (1966), the brain behind the term, Development Support Communication (DSC) describes it as development planning and implementation in which more adequate action is taken on human behavioural factors in the design of development projects and their objectives. Development communication and development support communication are thus two different terms. Development Communication, communicates developmental messages to people for the betterment of their economic and social status and conditions, whereas Development Support Communication addresses the developmental planning and the plan of operation for implementation.

We can say that Development Support Communication is a map or blueprint that shows the path and leads us to the development goals. The practice of Development Support Communication, (DSC) is a multi-sectorial process of information sharing, about development agendas and planned actions. It links planners, beneficiaries and implementers of development actions, including the donor community.

In short, DSC is a legitimate function of development planning and implementation. DSC therefore needs to be examined as a valuable (technology) tool for using in the social communication process to foster and strengthen sustainable development at local and national levels.

It is a strategised activity aimed to bring purposive changes in a society to improve its socio economic conditions. DSC makes use of all possible and available means and structures of information sharing. It is certainly limited to the mass media alone. To ensure its maximum efficiency, it uses both formal and informal channels of communication, such as the youth and women's associations, public places like markets, churches, meetings and festivals and peoples gatherings.

There are some factors which are considered as the basic ingredients for Development Support Communication. If these factors are worked out in a positive direction, then they will surely contribute to the development of the respective country in all aspects and sectorial levels. We can say that apart from attaining primary targets and goals for development, these secondary targets or factors need to be achieved so that the journey of a nation on the road of development could be made easy. These factors are also termed as 'An Extension Approach' as these serve as a value added feature to the base concept of development.

Some of these factors are listed as follows:

Health: For me, health is an abstract topic. It may bear different meanings for different people. The most relevant definition of health is that which has been given by World Health Organisation (WHO). According to WHO, health is defined as 'a state of complete physical, mental and social well-being and not merely the absence of disease and infirmity'. However this definition is a contradiction according to other experts and authorities.

The word 'complete' in the definition is not justified because even if someone is not ill, and is absolutely fit, still there is a scope of betterment and improvement and advancement. So it is operationally not possible to attain a 'complete' (100 per cent) physical, mental and social well-being status. In addition there are other dimensions of health that are not considered in this definition such as sexual, emotional and spiritual health. Even after so much of criticism, this definition is the most enduring one.

The Indian Perspective on Health

Let me provide you with the policies and programmes introduced by Government of India in health sector.

National Anti-Malaria Programme (1953), National Leprosy Control Programme (1995), Urban Malaria Scheme (1971), National Cancer Control Programme (1975; 1985), National AIDS Control

Programme (1987; 1999), National TB Control Programme (1962; 1992), National Iodine Deficiency Disorders Control Programme (1992), Pilot Project on Oral Health (1995), National and District Mental Health Programme (1996), National Dengue Control Programme and National Surveillance Programme for Communicable Diseases (1997) and National Immunisation Programmes.

As a result of these policies and programmes India has witnessed a remarkable boost and improvement in the health sector. Some of the achievements are as follows:

Reduced crude birth rate (CBR) from 40.8 (1951) to 26.4 (1998, SRS); Halved the infant mortality rate (IMR) from 146 per 1000 live births in 1951 to 70 per 1000 live births in 1999 (MoHRD, 2002); Quadrupled couple protection rate (CPR) from 10.4 per cent (1971) to 44 per cent (1999); Reduced crude death rate (CDR) from 25 (1951) to 9.0 (1998, SRS); Added 25 years to life expectancy from 37 years to 62 years; Nearly achieved a universal awareness of the need for and methods of family planning, and Reduced total fertility rate from 6.0 (1951) to 3.3 (1997, SRS). (*Source*: National Population Policy 2000b and MoHRD 2000).

Number of reported cases of polio has progressively decreased from 28757 in 1987 to 3265 in 1995 to 1005 reported during 1996. In 2000, only 265 cases had been detected throughout the country. Most parts of the country have become polio-free and widespread transmission is restricted only to the states of Bihar and Uttar Pradesh. A review of the TB programme undertaken in February 2000 by the government and WHO found that there has been a striking increase in the proportion of patients cured. Number of malaria cases has declined from 75 million in 1951 to 2.2 million in 2000. Number of leprosy cases per 10,000 people has decreased from 38.1 in 1951 to 3.74 in 2000. The HIV estimates for the year 2001 (based on HIV Sentinel Surveillance round-2001) reveals that while the AIDS epidemic is still spreading there is a gradual decline in new infections. The number of new infections can be put to a figure of 0.11 million compared to 0.16 million in 2000. Small pox and guinea worm have been eradicated.

National Rural Health Mission (NRHM): National Rural Health Mission (launched in April 2005) is the health programme initiated by

Government of India for improving the health care and delivery across rural India. This programme is of great importance to the Indian health development scenario. The NRHM focused especially on 18 states with poor infrastructure and low public health indicators, namely Bihar, Jharkhand, Madhya Pradesh, Chhattisgarh, Uttar Pradesh, Rajasthan, Odhisa, Uttarakhand, Assam, Arunachal Pradesh, Manipur, Mizoram, Meghalaya, Nagaland, Sikkim, Tripura, Himachal Pradesh and Jammu and Kashmir. This scheme also aims at improving sanitation and hygiene infrastructure across India.

The programme aimed at strengthening state health systems with a special focus on Reproductive and Child Health (RCH) services and Disease Control Programmes. Though largely restricted to rural areas, components such as RCH services and entitlement such as Janani Suraksha Yojna (JSY) and the Janani Shishu Suraksha Karyakram (JSSK) were extended to urban areas as well.

One of the key components of the NRHM is to provide every village in the country with a trained female community health activist ASHA or Accredited Social Health Activist. Selected from the village itself and accountable towards it, the ASHA activist will be trained to work as an interface between the community and the public health system.

There is also a Village Health, Sanitation and Nutrition Committee (VHSNC) working under NRHM which creates awareness about nutritional issues and significance of nutrition as an important determinant of health. It may act as a grievances cum its redressal forum on health and nutrition issues.

Another committee named as Rogi Kalyan Samiti (Patient Welfare Committee) or the Hospital Management Society is a simple yet effective management structure. This committee, which would be a registered society, acts as a group of trustees for the hospitals to manage the affairs of the hospital. It consists of members from the local Panchayati Raj Institutions (PRIs), NGOs, local elected representatives and officials from the Government sector who are responsible for proper functioning and management of the hospital, Community Health Centre, FRUs. The RKS or HMS are free to prescribe, generate and use the funds they have as per their best judgment for the smooth functioning and maintenance of the quality of services.

The goals of NRHM (as given on their official website) in the 12th Five Year Plan are as under:

Reduction of MMR (Maternal Mortality Rate) to <100 per 100000 live births; Reducing IMR (Infant Mortality Rate) to <27 per 1000 live births; Reduction in NMR (Neonatal Mortality Rate) to <18 per 1000 live births; Reducing TFR (Total Fertility Rate) to 2.1; Elimination of Filaria—in all the 250 districts, Kala-azar in all 514 blocks and leprosy in all districts; Reduction in TB prevalence and mortality by 50 per cent; Reduction in annual Malaria incidence to <1/1000 pop.; Reduction in JE (Japanese Encephalitis, a disease caused by the mosquito-borne Japanese encephalitis virus) mortality by 50 per cent; Sustaining case fatality rate of less than 1 per cent for dengue.

Other than these programmes and policies, there are several other departments which are contributing to the well-being of India's health sector. Some of them are as follows:

Department of AYUSH: Department of Indian Systems of Medicine and Homoeopathy (ISM&H) was created in March 1995 and renamed as Department of Ayurveda, Yoga and Naturopathy, Unani, Siddha and Homoeopathy (AYUSH) in November 2003 with a view for providing focused attention to the development of education and research in Ayurveda, Yoga and Naturopathy, Unani, Siddha and Homoeopathy systems. The department continued to lay emphasis on upgrading the department of AYUSH with respect to educational standards, quality control and standardisation of drugs, improving the availability of medicinal plant material, research and development and awareness generation about the efficacy of these systems domestically and internationally.

Objectives of this department:

To upgrade the educational standards in the Indian system of Medicines and Homoeopathy colleges in the country. To strengthen existing research institutions and ensure a time-bound research programme on identified diseases for which these systems have an effective treatment. To draw up schemes for promotion, cultivation and regeneration of medicinal plants used in these systems, To evolve the Pharmacopoeiaof standards for Indian Systems of Medicine and Homoeopathy drugs.

Jan Aushadhi: This is an important initiative taken by Department of Pharmaceuticals, Government of India. Under this initiative, many Jan Aushadhi stores were set up across the country where unbranded generic drugs are being sold at lesser prices but they were equivalent in quality and efficiency just as the expensive branded drugs.

This campaign was implemented with the help of Pharma CPSUs (HAL, IDPL, BCPL, RDPL and KAPL) and with the support of State Governments. The first Jan Aushadhi store was opened in the country at a Civil Hospital, in Amritsar, with the support and co-operation of the State Government of Punjab. More Jan Aushadhi stores were set up in Delhi, Haryana, Rajasthan, Andhra Pradesh and Punjab. Other states also showed keen interest in opening such stores and these stores were opened in other districts too.

The Department of Pharmaceuticals is actively engaged in providing appropriate assistance in expanding this venture to other parts of the country as well. This initiative is ensuring quality of medicines at affordable prices to all and furthering the cause of affordable health care for each and every citizen of the country.

Below are a few key points regarding health which should be understood by you in order to clearly understand the concept.

Health is a complex concept and it is difficult to define; Many different definitions and understandings of it exist. Understandings of health differ according to experience and expertise. Factors such as age, social class and gender have an impact on these. Theoretical perspectives about health can aids our understandings of the subjective health experience. A common man's understanding and an expert understandings of health may differ but both are central to developing the understandings about what health is, how it may be explored and how it may be maintained.

Health therefore is a pre-requisite for development. A healthy mind and body leads to a healthy life, through processes and initiates an efficient action plan which ultimately pushes a community or country or an individual towards development. Hence, health is an important factor in the Development Support Communication framework.

Empowerment: Empowerment a multi-dimensional social process that helps people gain control over their own lives. Empowerment refers to increasing the spiritual, political, social, educational, gender, or economic strength of individuals and communities. It is a process that fosters power in the people for using in their own lives, their communities and in their societies, by acting and enacting on the issues that they define as important.

Empowerment is a process that challenges our assumptions about the way things are and can be. It challenges our basic assumptions about power, helping, achieving, and succeeding. It is the process of enhancing the capacity of individuals or groups to make choices and to transform those choices into desired actions and outcomes. The World Bank's 2002 Empowerment Sourcebook identified empowerment as 'the expansion of assets and capabilities of poor people to participate in, negotiate with, influence, control, and hold accountable institutions that affect their lives.'

The concept of empowerment lies within the central core idea of establishing the 'power'; the power which enables an individual or a community or a nation to hold its best possible capabilities in order to use them (the power) to enjoy the fruits of their desired actions.

Women Empowerment: Before I make you understand what women empowerment actually means, let me give you the concrete and bitter facts that justify the urgency and the need for increasing the empowerment for the women section in the world and hence in India too.

*Of the 1.3 billion people who live in absolute poverty around the globe, 70 per cent are women. For these women, poverty doesn't just mean scarcity and want. It means rights denied, opportunities curtailed and voices silenced. Consider the following:

- Women work two-thirds of the world's working hours, according to the United Nations Millennium Campaign, to halve worlds poverty by the year 2015. The overwhelming majority of the labor that sustains life like–growing food, cooking, raising children, caring for the elderly, maintaining a house, hauling water—are all done by women, and universally this work is accorded with a low status and no pay. The ceaseless cycle of labor rarely shows up in the economic analyses of a society's production and value.

• Women earn only 10 per cent of the world's income. Where women work for money, they may be limited to a set of jobs deemed suitable for women—invariably which are low-paying, and hold low-status positions.

• Women own less than 1 per cent of the world's property. Where laws or customs prevent women from owning land or other productive assets, from getting loans or credit, or from having the right to inheritance or to own their home, they have no assets to leverage for economic stability and cannot invest in their own or their children's futures.

• Women make up two-thirds of the estimated 876 million adults worldwide who cannot read or write; and girls make up 60 per cent of the 77 million children not attending primary school. Education is among the most important drivers of human development—women who are educated have fewer children than those who are denied schooling (some studies correlate each additional year of education with a 10 per cent drop in fertility). They delay their first pregnancies, have healthier children (each additional year of schooling a woman has is associated with a 5 to 10 per cent decline in child deaths, according to the United Nations Population Fund).

Around the globe, home and community are not safe havens for a billion girls and women: At least one in three females on earth has been physically or sexually abused, often repeatedly and often by a relative or acquaintance. By the World Bank's estimate, violence rivals cancer as a cause of morbidity and mortality in the case of women of childbearing age. Even within the marriage, women may not be able to negotiate when and what type of sex to have, nor to protest their husbands' multiple sex partners. Poverty and exclusion push some girls and women to engage into sex work, almost always the desperate, last choice of people without other choices.

Data in this section is drawn from organizations that collect and aggregate information at a global level, including the U.N.; Millennium Campaign, the World Bank, UNICEF, UNESCO, the U.N. Population Fund, the World Health Organization, the U.S. Department of State and Department of Health and Human Services.

It's quite clear from the above listed facts that women sector across the globe is suffering and is being kept deprived of legitimate opportunities in order to be developed. This essentially catalyses the need and urgency of the establishment of proper women empowerment policies and schemes throughout the world. Development of society in its real sense is absolutely unthinkable, without equal participation of the women in each and every aspect of life. Take a look to understand what women empowerment actually refers to and the missions and schemes for the empowerment of women in our country.

Women empowerment simply refers to increasing the spiritual, political, social, educational, gender or economic strength of the women so that they can gain a sound and better control over their lives. Women empowerment policies essentially governs the enabling of all women to negotiate their freedoms and increase their capabilities in all aspects of life.

The condition of most of the women in India are not good as it is required to be. Even in this era of the 21st century, more than 50 per cent of the women in India are being ruled by men. Since the birth of the Indian social culture (dates back to 5000 years ago) the male has been dominating over women. Women are being kept deprived of the valid opportunities, facilities, education, rights and social recognition to which they are legitimately entitled.

To ensure betterment and to promote all round development of women, Ministry of Women and Child Development, Government of India launched The National Mission for Empowerment of Women (NMEW) on International Women's Day in 2010. NMEW is aimed to strengthen an overall processes that promotes all-round Development of Women.

It has the mandate to strengthen the inter-sector convergence; facilitate the process of coordinating all the women's welfare and socioeconomic development programmes across ministries and departments. The Mission aims to provide a single window service for all programmes run by the government for women under the aegis of various central ministries.

In light with its mandate, the Mission has been named Mission Poorna Shakti, implying a vision for holistic empowerment of women. The National Resource Centre for Women has been set up which functions as a national convergence centre for all schemes and programmes for women. It acts as a central repository of knowledge, information, research and data on all gender related issues and is the main body servicing the National and State Mission Authority.

Apart from NMEW, there are many NGOs, trade unions, Self Help Groups across the country which contribute a lot in empowerment of women in India. One of the main trade unions for women in India is SEWA. SEWA stands for Self Employed Women's Association which was registered in year 1972. SEWA was founded by a prominent civil rights leader, Dr. Ela Bhatt. Its headquarter is located in Ahmedabad, Gujarat. SEWA is strongly supported by the World Bank which holds it out as a model to be replicated elsewhere.

It is an organisation of poor, self-employed women workers. These are women who earn a living through their own labour or small businesses. They do not obtain regular salaried employment with welfare benefits like workers in the organised sector. They are the unprotected labour force of our country. Constituting, 93 per cent of the labour force, these are workers of the unorganised sector. Of the female labour force in India, more than 94 per cent are in the unorganised sector. However their work is not counted and hence remains invisible.

SEWA's main goals are to organise women workers for any employment whereby workers obtain work security, income security, food security and social security (at least health care, child care and shelter). SEWA works on organising women employment to ensure that every family obtains full employment.

Women who are associated with SEWA feel self-reliant and empowered as they are being exposed to newer opportunities and capabilities.

Literacy and Education: Literacy and education are two different concepts but are often used together. One needs to understand the fine line of difference between these two terms. Literacy is essentially the ability to read and write. Literacy, as defined in Indian Census operations, is the ability to read and write with the understanding in any language. A person who can merely read but cannot write is not classified as a literate. Any formal education or minimum educational standard is not necessary to be considered literate. Whereas education is a form of advanced learning in which knowledge, habits and skills (about any particular aspect) are given or taken through research, teaching or training. Technically, literacy is the initial stage of education. One has to be a literate in order to be educated (officially).

To me, literacy is not the simple reading of words or a set of associated symbols and sounds, but an act of critical understanding of the situation in the world. Literacy is not an end in itself but a means of extending individual efforts towards education, involving overall interdisciplinary responses to his problems. Literacy leads to education and results in empowerment with the acquisition of the essential knowledge and skills, which enable one to engage in activities, required for effective functioning of the individual in his group and community and use these skills towards his own and his community's development.

Literacy is now part of the Human Rights Dialogue. Now most of the nations of the world have also accepted their obligation towards providing at least free elementary education to their citizens. Article 26 of the Universal Declaration of Human Rights declares:

"Everyone has the right to education. Education shall be free, at least in the elementary and fundamental stages. Elementary education shall be compulsory. Technical and Professional education shall be generally available and higher education shall be equally accessible to all on the basis of merit".

This Right is also repeated in the UN Declaration of the Rights of the Child which seeks to ensure "Right to free and compulsory education at least in the elementary stages and education to promote general culture, abilities, judgment and sense of responsibility to become a useful member of society and opportunity to recreation, and play to attain the same purpose as of education".

India has ratified the above right, and these therefore have the power of domestic laws. From the Human Rights perspective, constitutional guarantees arise automatically.

Department of School Education and Literacy, under Ministry of Human Resource Development, Government of India gives an overview of the role of education as follows:

The essence and role of education articulated in the National Policy on Education (NPE), 1986/92 continues to be relevant even 25 years after its formulation. NPE states:

In our national perception education is essentially for all. This is fundamental to our all-round development.

Education has an acculturating role. It refines sensitivities and perceptions that contribute to national cohesion, a scientific temper and independence of mind and spirit—thus furthering the goals of socialism, secularism and democracy enshrined in our Constitution.

Education develops manpower for different levels of the economy. It is also the substrate on which research and development flourish, being the ultimate guarantee of national self-reliance.

In sum, education is a unique investment in the present and the future. This cardinal principle is the key to the National Policy on Education.

In 2010 the country achieved a historic milestone when Article 21-A and the Right of Children to Free and Compulsory Education (RTE) Act, 2009 became operative on 1st April 2010. The enforcement of Article 21-A and the RTE Act represented a momentous step forward in our country's struggle for universalizing elementary education. The RTE Act was anchored in the belief that the values of equality, social justice and democracy and the creation of a just and humane society can be achieved only through provision of inclusive elementary education to all.

In keeping with the vision of providing education of equitable quality to fully harness the nation's human potential, the department has laid down the following objectives to:

Reinforce the national and integrative character of education in partnership with the States/Union Territories; Improve quality and standards of school education and literacy towards building a society committed to constitutional values; Universalize elementary education in keeping with the rights conferred under the RTE Act; Universalize opportunities for quality secondary education; Establish a fully literate society.

These objectives are intended to be accomplished through the following major programmes of the department:

Elementary level: Sarva Shiksha Abhiyan (SSA) and Mid-Day Meal (MDM); Secondary level: Rashtriya Madhyamik Shiksha Abhiyan (RMSA), Model Schools, Vocational Education, Girls' Hostel, Inclusive Education for the Disabled, ICT@School; Adult Education: Saakshar Bharat; Teacher Education: Schemes for strengthening teacher education; Women's education: Mahila Samakhya; Minority Education: Scheme for Providing Quality Education in Madarsas (SPQEM); Infrastructure Development of Minority Institutions (IDMI)

The Department endeavors to:

Provide free and compulsory education to all children at elementary level; Become a partner with the States and Union Territories to reinforce the national and integrative character of education; Build a society committed to Constitutional values with the help of quality school education and literacy; Universalise opportunities for quality secondary education.

In order to make the dream of secondary education a reality for every deserving student in the country, the Department's objectives are clearly marked. It has to:

Increase access to quality school education by expanding the network of schools, through existing as well as new institutions; Bring equity to the system of secondary education by including disadvantaged groups as well as the weaker sections, who were kept deprived hitherto; Ensure quality and improved standards of education by supporting the existing institutions and facilitating setting up of new ones; Initiate policy-level changes in terms of institutional and systematic reforms, which further create a world-class secondary education curriculum that is able to generate brilliance among the children.

[In my opinion, one does not essentially need to be literate in order to be educated. What I personally think is, if a person is aware or rather holds an experience regarding any specific aspect of life which ultimately changes the way he is used to think, then the person is well educated. Education could be in any field; nobody can cage the definition and meaning of education. It means different things to different people and has no upper limits of understanding. For example, in rural areas, elderly people are mostly illiterate. Though they do not even know how to read or write their own names, yet they are so well experienced that they guide the entire village and cater every individual who wishes to seek their 'expert' advices on any issue. This means they are educated or I would say well educated as compared to other 'literate' people in the community. Another example is seen in our daily life, kids and youngsters are so well equipped with the knowledge and skills when it comes to dealing with any new gadget or gizmo. A formally educated person, even after doing PhD is not able to access or understand the mechanism of these technical gadgets. So it would not be wrong to consider these kids educated, when it comes to these technologies! Therefore one does not necessarily need to be literate in order to be educated.]

Water Harvesting: Water harvesting is a management technique for accumulating and depositing water (essentially rainwater) for reuse, before it goes into the ground or aquifer (an underground layer of water bearing permeable rock or unconsolidated materials from which ground water can be extracted using a water well). The harvested rainwater can be used for domestic purposes such as irrigation, gardening, washing clothes and utensils, for livestock etc. it can also be used as drinking water (with a little treatment, if required) if the storage is a tank or a closed container which can be accessed and cleaned when one needs to do so.

Water is essentially the most important life supporting natural element on earth. Without water life is simply unthinkable. Our earth is the only planet which has life and it is all because of the availability of water in it.

By the year 2020, says a World Bank report, most major Indian cities will run dry. India's supply of water is also rapidly dwindling primarily due to mismanagement of water resources, although over-pumping and pollution are also significant contributors. Water shortage can hinder the agricultural, economic and social growth and development of the country. Water harvesting can easily ease out the problem of water shortage in our country and other parts of the globe. In fact, water harvesting promotes energy conservation and can be an alternative way to check depletion of the water table.

Surplus water from harvesting can be efficiently used to recharge the ground water. Rain water harvesting is being practiced on a regular basis in the states of Tamil Nadu, Kerala, Maharashtra (Pune only) and Rajasthan (Thar Desert area) in India.

The most common technique used for harvesting rainwater is roof top collection. In this process rainwater is collected from the roof (when it rains) and it is then sent to the storage tank through a pipeline. The other new technique for collecting rainwater is the inverted umbrella technique. In this technique, rain water is collected using an inverted umbrella shaped dish. This dish serves as a big bowl for collecting that rainwater.

Apart from these two techniques, a pit, well, pavement or a digging may be used to collect and store rainwater.

10

Message Design for Development Communication

Message design for development communication is the process of conceiving, processing and packaging the message in an efficient way so that it can be communicated to the target audience. It is a system based approach in which messages are designed in a single integrated process rather than a series of discrete attempts or efforts. Message designing for communication is a strategy and research based approach for creating the desired message which is to be communicated to a specific group of people.

It encompasses all forms of audio and visual communication approaches and practices such as, graphic designing, typography, editing, web designing, animation, illustration, copywriting, advertising, professional writing etc.

The main aim of designing the message for effective communication for development is to seek the attention of the receiver so that it can attract, create desires, inspire, motivate people to respond to the messages in order to make a favorable impact on them regarding the respective message content.

The message which is intended to be communicated for the development has to be effective. The entire development approach is primarily based on the messages which are aimed to provide a holistic view of development project objectives and resources. Following points should be kept in mind by a development communicator while designing messages for development:

Timeliness: Messages should be synchronised with the timing of the events/activities they have intended to influence and cover. For example, a development message which is related to a specific agriculture crop should be delivered at the suitable time i.e., not too early or after the season or event.

Usefulness/Importance of Content: Messages should portray their usefulness and importance to the people. Unless and until people see the relative benefit and advantage in accepting the new message or idea or method, their chances of getting interested in the messages are rare.

Appropriateness: Messages should be appropriate and logical in content for what they convey. People should recognise the appropriateness of the message so that they can decide what is suitable for their individual condition. For example; if a new technology is to be adopted, the people must be explained the reasons and facts for giving up the old ones and adopting the new one.

Simplicity: Simplicity of messages allow the people and receivers at grass root levels to understand it easily. Easy understanding of messages helps in better realisation and adoption of development messages.

Potential threats and hindrances in the process of message designing for development:

Production Team Related Factors: The knowledge and attitude of the production team towards a particular topic and audiences affects the standard and quality of production efforts. The producers of the messages should be unbiased and objective, having better analytical skills so as to maintain the effectiveness of the message.

Content Related Factors: The content of the messages should be based on the assessment of the needs and consumption habits of the people. Without this initial research and assessment, messages will seem to be less important or appropriate to the audiences and people will not easily agree with it.

Media Related Factors: The Development Communicator should know about the media habits of the people. Appropriateness of media for the content is very essential for dissemination of messages intending to bring about any change.

Audience Related Factors: Lack of media literacy, visual literacy and ignorance can lead to the lack of communication. Different people have different attitude towards the medium, which may lead to differences in individual exposure, choices, retention and comprehension of messages.

Context Related Factors: A suitable environment is required for any development communication project. These projects, in order to maintain their effectiveness, require the support of political leadership, economic power and cultural authorities such as religious and cultural groups.

11

Role of Mass Media in Development

The need for channels of mass communication for communicating, has been of paramount since the evolution of modern human civilisation on the earth. Mass media or channels of mass communication quantitatively, amplify the reach of the messages; enhance the proximity factor between the communicator and receivers, thus enabling the communicator to maximise the impact of the messages. It is said that information is power. Mass media helps in the dissemination of this 'power', which sets the base for empowerment of the receivers. This empowerment eventually contributes a lot towards development of a nation in each and every aspect and sector. The role of mass media in many countries like India has been very notable.

The basic idea about the importance of mass media in national the development is wrapped up on a central concept that people can be influenced and persuaded by the messages that come from the mass media. Though mass media has been subjected to a lot of criticism in last 20 years, yet it is a facts that mass media played a dynamic role in the modernisation of an individual and it is the central force in the wake of the development process, and are accepted by all communication experts.

A remarkable personality in the field of communication, Daniel Lerner proposed a model: "Urbanization - Literacy - Media Growth and Participation - Political Participation". Lerner postulated four dependent factors existing one after another in the society's growth towards modernisation. He proposed that, even before mass media can accumulate or materialise itself, there must be first of all the urbanisation stage followed by the literacy stage. After which there is mass growth and participation, modern development will be greatly enhanced, which in turn determines political participation and ultimately this will take a nation, one step further towards development. Thus, Lerner has glorified the role of mass media and communication as the determinants of politics.

Another great expert in the field of communication is Everett M. Rogers, who ascribed mass media with the status of it being a 'magic' in its capabilities. According to the model proposed by Rogers, antecedent variables such as literacy, education, social status, age, cosmopolitan standards when exposed to mass media becomes consequent variables of empathy, agriculture and home innovativeness, political knowledge, action, achievement motivation and educational and occupational aspirations.

The functions and role of mass media in the development is so important that Wilbur Schramm put forward a list of possible 'functions' of mass media, as being the watchmen or check against unwanted elements or infringements of rights; to help in the decision making policies; as a teacher; or help to widen horizons; focus attention; raise aspirations; frees people from feudalism; establishing a favourable climate for change; help indirectly and directly to change strongly held attitudes; strengthen interpersonal channels; confer status; bring common people into the process of decision making; enforce social norms and taste; helps in formation of national identity; can help in teaching through audio visual aids, thus theoretically, a wide range of utilisation is possible.

Apart from this, Lasswell quotes that the mass media can survey the environment; correlate parts of the society and transmit cultural and social heritage from one generation to the next.

In my opinion, mass media is a potential force and an omnipotent tool through which contents in the form of messages and information is communicated and as soon as its audience is exposed to or is accessible to its contents, the message will automatically change the individual's attitude and behavior accordingly. That's when Marshall McLuhan talks about this in "The Medium is the Message" ("The medium is the message" is a phrase coined by Marshall McLuhan meaning that the form of a medium embeds itself in the message, creating a symbiotic relationship by which the medium influences how the message is perceived).

The performance of mass media has been criticised on the basis that there are certain limitations of mass media such as: limitations of coverage and supply of the mass media. It is to be found in every country in the world but has not reached the same level of development in all countries. Because of these reasons a communicator cannot make full use of mass media. Also, there is limited funding to the purchase of equipments required for mass communication in developing and/or underdeveloped countries. Illiteracy in developing and underdeveloped countries is another major factor which hinders the impact of mass media and makes it a nullified means.

A remarkably high number of people and communication analysts and economists are in favor of spending the money or fund in providing basic facilities to the people in the underdeveloped nations. According to them, the money which is supposed to be spent in establishing and purchasing mass media equipment and organizing the whole mass communication framework, should be funded in fulfilling the basic needs of the poor people living in developing and underdeveloped or the Third World countries.

Let's discuss the role and performance of mass media like Print Media, TV, Radio and Outdoor Media in national development.

Print Media: Print industry of India is the largest in the world with over 100 million copies of newspapers, magazines and journals being sold every day. Print media is the oldest means of mass communication in India. It has a remarkable background as it was associated with the people ever since the time of freedom struggle of our country. Many leaders from Gandhi and downwards used their newspapers to initiate the people to participate in the freedom struggle. Political leaders used the press to rouse the people. Newspapers always had the sword of Damocles hanging over the head of the British rulers.

In India print media has a rich pedigree of being a witness and a catalyst to the birth and growth of the nation. After the independence of India there has been a phenomenal rise in the number of newspapers and their circulation. Press has become an important ingredient required for social change. Even after the advent of new media (internet) and electronic media, the legacy of print media is maintained and increasing day by day. Print media is keeping the public intact and integrated to each other. Technological advancements and innovations in the print industry have made newspapers and journals more interesting. It reaches every nook and corner of the country. From a rag picker to a multi-millionaire, everyone has access to the newspaper. The main cause of existence of the newspaper in India is the effective communication impact it has on the public. Newspapers are being published in Hindi, English and local languages and dialects. This makes people think that they are also associated with the nation's progress and development. Language is the major factor of national integrity and harmony. Language of a nation is the most powerful tool which keeps the people living in it united. People in India get to know about policies, cases, schemes, news, and information of regional, national and international importance. Print media helps people in shaping their opinion regarding anything. This makes them aware and empowered and helps them to make the right choice to make their lives better. Ultimately this empowerment leads to the development of the nation. Hence it is clear that print media has the lions share in the development and development communication of India and other developing countries across the globe.

Radio: Radio emerged after the establishment of print industry in India. Since then, radio is playing its notable role in communication for development. It is a cheap means of mass communication and almost every Indian can own a radio set. The most important feature of radio as a communication device is its versatile nature when it comes to language and dialects. Radio stations in different states of India have programmes in their own language. Local people can understand whatever is being broadcasted on radio. Also, there is a large variety and many options to choose any type of programme in any language. Unlike any static information sources like, TV, computer (internet), radio is portable. One can carry a radio handset in his pocket and can listen to it on the go without any difficulty. The tone of the announcer, or the RJ in most of the radio programmes is kept conversational so that listeners feel as if they are personally associated with the show.

The radio (All India Radio) covers over 99 per cent of the total land area of India, which is the highest among all means of mass communication in the country. It is also the world's largest broadcasting network. Radio is an important medium for knowing about all important events and happenings in the country and outside the country. AIR covers the live elections and provides its bulletins. It also covers live sports and special events. It broadcasts news services in all major language. Radio services are a very active medium of communication during natural calamities. Radio develops the efficiency of making the right choice followed by the desired action in the people by making them aware. This ultimately pushes us toward development; hence radio shares a major chunk of appreciation in the Indian development scenario.

Television: TV in India has been in existence for more than forty years from now. But it has come to the forefront only in the past two decades and more so in the recent past. During the early 1980s, colored television was introduced by state owned broadcaster Doordarshan (DD) timed with the Asian Games which India hosted in 1982. In the early 1990s, satellite television broadcasting by foreign programmers like CNN followed by STAR TV and a little later by domestic channels such as Zee TV, Sun TV fuelled the purchase of the TV sets all across the country.

Television today is playing the most important role in the development of India. It is playing the role of a facilitator in the process of holistic development in India and is being acknowledged everywhere. The government in India and the Third World countries have used the tools of mass media to create awareness about their welfare policies. Indian television industry along with Indian press has been making contributions towards social development. Some of the stated objectives of Prasar Bharti are:

1. Inform freely, truthfully and objectively the citizens of India on all matters of public interests, national and international interests.

2. Provide adequate coverage to the diverse cultures and languages of the various regions of the country through appropriate programmes in the regional languages and dialects.

3. Promote social justice, national consciousness, national integration, communal harmony and the upliftment of women.

4. Pay special attention to the fields of education and spread literacy, agriculture, rural development, environment, health and family welfare and science and technology.

TV is the most influential medium of mass communication. As it is audio visual medium, it made an everlasting impact on the viewers. People start believing what is being shown on TV channels. Not only in urban areas but people in rural India are also being benefited by TV. Special programmes related towards the farmers, doctors, teachers and students in rural areas are helping them to learn new ways and skills to improve their working. Daily soaps on TV channels play a prominent impact on urban and rural population reflecting and showing day to day problems in a typical Indian society and/or family and their solutions to it.

Television has an all pervasive influence on its audiences and is a big source of information, knowledge, news, motivations, aspirations and innovativeness to the people who watch it. Hence it helps the people in making the right choice followed by right actions which ultimately brings social development in the country.

Outdoor Media and Publicity: Apart from TV, radio and print media in India, outdoor publicity has a great importance in communication and development. We almost every day find ourselves engaged with such kind of outdoor publicity media while travelling in a bus, metro, rail or even when we are in our personal conveyance (at signals, banners on road side). Outdoor publicity through advertising, banners, posters, transit media grabs the attention of the public and mobilises or changes their behaviour and thought patterns towards that very issue, product or service. Hence, outdoor media plays a key role in development of the society.

12

Role of Traditional Media in Development

Though mass media like radio, TV, newspaper etc. reaches every nook and corner of the country yet there is a need for the channels of communication which can approach and cater rural population (72 per cent) efficiently. When it comes to approaching the rural public personally (interpersonally) the use of the traditional media becomes essential. Many a times, due to some unforeseen circumstances and factors mass media fails to prove its efficiency in remote and rural areas. In that case, traditional media legitimately proves its legacy. Traditional media like music, drama, dance, puppetry, street play, fairs and festivals have a very notable role in communication and development. These media are appreciated very much in the villages of India. Its approaches to the rural population is in a more explicit way as compared to any other media. Fairs, festivals, shows and street plays are very important when it comes to sharing views, ideas, information, culture and economy. People in rural areas tend to socialize through these media. Traditional media empowers and maintain cultural and beliefs and practices among the people in rural India. It imposes a feeling of commonality between them. Small gatherings, meetings and group discussions (*choupal*) are other ways of sharing and communicating in villages. People of all age groups, from kids to youngsters to the elderly people learn and adopt quickly from traditional media. This is the reason why government and other social organisations organize street plays, drama, folk dances and fairs to inform, educate and persuade rural people on personal basis to make them aware of the welfare policies meant for them. Therefore traditional media has a great role in the development of the nation.

13

Cyber Media and Development

The 21st century is the era of cyber media and digital technology. With the advent of this new media (internet, mobiles etc.) the spirit of cyber media has been strengthened a lot. Following are the ways in which cyber media is proving itself to be a master piece in national development.

E Governance: It means electronic governance. Governance in simple words is to govern, or to manage. It refers to the decisions that define expectations, grant power or verify performance. Thus, electronic governance means governance driven by technology. When information and communication technologies (ICTs) are applied for delivering government services, exchange of information communication transactions, integration of various standalone systems between government to citizens, government to business or government to government platforms; E governance emerges out. E governance encompasses the use of technologies that help the governing party as well as the party which is to be governed. It is a transparent and non-partial system of delivering or gaining or sharing information, products and services.

The main concept the E governance is to reach to the beneficiary and ensure that the services intended to reach the desired individual or group has been met with. E governance refines the channels and cuts down the unwanted layers of interference while delivering governmental services. The beneficiary is directly linked with the government without any interference of middlemen or brokers, and hence gets the first hand direct information and services. E governance is the best possible way to form a corruption free government. Many countries of the world are looking forward to expand and modify the aura of governance to ensure development and betterment. It is the future.

People always get confused between E governance and E government. These two terms more or less refers to the same concept, but with a little difference. E government is the use of ICT in public administration in order to improve public services and democratic processes and to strengthen its support to the public. It is defined as 'the employment of the internet and the world wide web for delivering government information and services to the citizens'.

'E government essentially refers to 'the utilization of IT and ICT and other web based telecommunication technologies to improve and enhance the efficiency and effectiveness of service and delivery in the public sector'.

E government allows the public to be informed about what the government is working on as well as about the policies they are trying to implement. It has traditionally been understood as being cantered around the operations of the government. While E governance is understood to extend the scope by including the citizen's engagement and participation in governance. Thus, E government is a one way communication protocol while E governance is a two way communication protocol which consist of a citizen's participation along with the government.

Digital Democracy: Digital democracy can be defined as the pursuit and the practice of democracy in whatever view using digital media in online and offline political communication.

It is also termed as E democracy. E democracy is the use of information and communication technologies and strategies by democratic sectors within the political processes of local communities, states and regions, nations and on the global stage.

E democracy is connected with the use of information and communication technologies to engage citizens' support in the democratic decision-making processes and strengthen representative democracy.

Digital democracy, through internet provides a distinctive structure of opportunities that has the potential to renew interest in civic engagement and participations. Digital democracy is the direct democracy. The information available on internet allows people to become more knowledgeable about government and political issues, the interactivity allows for new forms of communication with government. The open posting of contact information, legislation agendas and policies makes government more transparent, potentially enabling more informed participation both online and offline.

E Choupals: E choupal is an initiative taken by the company ITC Limited to connect directly with rural farmers through internet for procurement of agricultural and aquaculture products like wheat, soyabean, coffee, prawns etc.

Under this programme computers with internet connection are installed in rural areas of India to offer farmers up-to-date marketing and agricultural information. Due to Echoupal, middlemen policy has been eliminated completely. Now farmers can directly negotiate the sale of their produce with ITC Limited. Internet access enables farmers to obtain information on *mandi* prices and good farming practices. They can also place orders for agricultural inputs like seeds and fertilizers. This improves the quality of the products farmers produce, and helps in obtaining a better price. Since the establishment of this initiative there has been a considerable rise in the income levels of the farmers due to rise in their yields, improvement in the quality of output and a fall in transaction and production costs.

Farmers can get the accurate and current information despite of their physical distance from the *mandis*. The information and knowledge got by the farmers from Echoupal is free of cost. Real time information and customized knowledge provided by the Echoupal enhances the ability of farmers to take decisions and align their farm output with market demand and secure quality and productivity. In short Echoupal is a one stop solution for all agriculture businesses in India.

Today Echoupal has empowered the lives of the people living in 10 states where 40,000 villages have 6500 Echoupals and around 4 million farmers have been benefited.

14

ICT and Development

ICT plays a great a role in the development of a nation. It explicitly opens up new opportunities and possibilities for the people living in developing or underdeveloped countries. Use of ICTs in different sectors viz., agriculture, economic, education, defense, health etc. has powered the development framework of all the countries in the world.

Information and Communication Technology for Development (ICT4D) refers to the use of information and communication technologies in the fields of socioeconomic development, international development and human rights. The concept behind this is that more and better information and communication furthers the development of a society by empowering its people and guides them to make better choice and judgement followed by the desired action directed towards the change for the betterment.

ICT is not just the use of technology for communication. It also requires an understanding of community developments, poverty, agriculture, healthcare and basic education, to use ICT efficiently. Needless to say that ICT has become an important part of our daily lives. It is widely used for various projects, policies, works and actions.

Let's go through the major uses of ICT in today's world:

ICT for weather, climate and emergency response activities: ICT is broadly used in weather forecasting now-a-days. Weather forecasting includes the use of mass media to update the public on weather reports. Weather satellites, Doppler radars, Automatic Weather Station (AWS), Wind profiler and other synoptic data or weather instruments are among the important monitoring devices used in weather forecasting. The use of ICT enables us to reduce the loss of life and property up to a great extent. People get to know about the weather and they get plenty of time to make plans or to tackle with the problems occurring due to adverse conditions. Also, in the time of calamities, we need ICT for disaster management. ICT helps in relief operations, providing early warnings and monitoring extreme weather events, supporting emergency response through communication and information sharing, supporting environmental, health and resource management activities.

ICT for people with disabilities: ICT can provide a whole new dimension to the lives of differently abled people in the world. It can give disabled people a powerful tool in their battle to gain employment. It integrates disabled people socially and economically into their communities. ICT also increases the skills, self-confidence and self-esteem of these people. Due to ICT, physical or functional barriers are eliminated up to a great extent, which enlarge the scope of activities available to disabled persons.

ICT for education: ICT has a great importance in imparting knowledge, education and information across the globe. It greatly facilitates the acquisition and absorption of knowledge, offering developing countries opportunities to enhance educational systems, improve policy formulation and widen the range of opportunities for setting up business and supporting the poor. Education has a vital role in addressing issues of poverty, gender equality and health in MDGs. This has led to the need of expanding the demand for education at all levels. ICT offeres an entire new range of possibilities to enhance the teaching and learning experience. It can enhance the quality of education by increasing the learners motivation and engagement by facilitating the acquisition of basic skills and by upgrading the teachers training which will eventually improve communication and exchange of information that will boost and empower economic and social development.

Today virtual classrooms and E classes are in vogue. There is no need of any school building or teacher to acquire education. ICT has led to the emergence of a new concept of 'boundary less classrooms'. As far as formal education is concerned, ICT has proved its legacy. Distance education programmes allows individuals to choose from any of the desired courses of their interest and level and get benefited by it. E classrooms in schools have made the boring and traditional methods (chalk and blackboard) of education, turn into an interesting and efficient learning experience.

ICT and livelihood: Most of the people around the world rely on agriculture to live sustainable lives. Agriculture provides our most basic human need which are food, clothing and shelter. Effective use of ICT has modified and advanced the information and technology sharing in the field of agriculture. Farmers are now able to take hold of updated information like prices, production techniques, services, storage and processing of the produced agricultural products. ICT can help to lessen the expenses of the poor farmers on resources like time, labor, energy and physical resources. This would have a great positive impact on their livelihood and incomes.

ICT can supply information to inform the policies, institutions, and processes that affect farmers' livelihood options. It also plays a great role in nurturing financial, natural, physical, human and social capital of these farmers. Due to initiatives like e choupal, farmers have access to the price, information, national and international markets. ICT increases production efficiency and creates conductive policy environment.

Apart from the contribution to these important sectors, ICTs are used for other sectors as well. Some of them are for E government, E governance, E business, E literacy, E health, E employment (virtual jobs), E environment (ICT is used as an instrument for environment protection and for promoting sustainable use of natural resources.), E security etc.

In recent years, ICT has been continuously used to generate the thrust in the effort to fight gender discrimination and to empower women. ICT builds marketable skills in women. These skills create alternative possibilities for income generation and the possibility of upward mobility. ICT increases the self-confidence and self-esteem in women allowing them to explore and travel more and develop a wider network of contacts. This travel and networking exposes them to the availability of more income opportunities. ICT opens new doors for education, communication and information sharing. It mobilises women's advocacy and interests groups. Education and information increases knowledge about the world and the political, economic, social and cultural factors that shape women's lives.

Thus, it is clear that ICT is touching each and every aspect of human life. It is the future of the world and if used wisely it can do wonders.

15

Case Studies

SITE: SITE stands for Satellite Instructional Television Experiment. It is one of the most extensive educational and social research project ever conducted in mass mediated communication. The effectiveness of TV as a medium for educating the masses in rural areas was emphasised by this experiment. With the help of international agencies like NASA, UNDP, ITU and UNESCO, ISRO succeeded in launching SITE on August 1, 1975.

The main objectives of the experiment were to educate the poor people of India on various issues via satellite broadcast media and also to help India gain technical experience in the field of satellite communications. The experiment ran for the period of one year from August 1, 1975 to July 31, 1976 covering more than 2400 villages in 20 districts of 6 states viz. Andhra Pradesh, Bihar, Karnataka, Madhya Pradesh, Orissa and Rajasthan.

The television programmes were produced by AIR and broadcasted by NASA's ATS-6 satellite stationed above India for the duration of the project. SITE also played a major role in helping develop India's own satellite programme INSAT. This project showed that India could use advanced technology to fulfillits socioeconomic needs of the country.

Under this project, 2 types of programmes were broadcasted; educational TV (ETV) and instructional TV (ITV). ETV programmes were designed for school kids and it focused on interesting and creative educational programmes. These programmes were broadcasted for one and half hours during school times. During holidays this time was used to broadcast teacher training programmes designed to train and guide almost 100,000 primary school teachers during the project duration. The ITV programmes were meant for adult audiences, mainly to those who were illiterate. Duration of these programmes was 2.5 hours during the evenings. ITV programmes catered to topics like health, hygiene, family planning, nutrition, improved practices in agriculture and events of national importance. Hence the programmes under SITE were broadcasted for 4 hours daily in 2 transmissions and in 4 languages - Hindi, Telugu, Oriya and Kannada.

TV sets were installed in schools and public community centers. Thousands of villagers gathered around the TV sets and watched the shows. SITE is one of the important factors contributing to the expansion of TV in India.

Water Harvesting by Rajendra Singh: Rajendra Singh is a well-known water conservationist from the Alwar district in the state of Rajasthan, in India. He was born on August 6, 1959 in Daula, Bagpat district, Uttar Pradesh. He was awarded the Ramon Magsaysay award for community leadership in 2001 for his extraordinary and pioneering work in community based efforts in water harvesting and water management. He is also known as 'Waterman of India'.

Rajendra is one of the members of the National Ganga River Basin Authority (NGRBA) under Ministry of Environment, Government of India. HGRBA was set up in 2009, as an empowered planning, financing, monitoring and coordinating authority for the Ganges in exercise of the power conferred under the Environment (protection) Act, 1986.

The Guardian named Rajendra Singh is one among the list of "50 people who could save the planet". Rajendra runs an NGO, Tarun Bharat Sangh (TBS) which was founded in 1975. Starting from a single village, over the years TBS helped build over 8600 Johads (earthen check dams and rainwater storage dams) and other water conservation structures to collect rain water for the dry season. This has brought water back in over 1000 villages and recharged five rivers in Rajasthan, named Aravari, Jahajwali, Ruparel, Sarsa and Bhagani. This technique of water conservation proposed by Rajendra is very effective and helpful for the people of the communities living close to Thar desert regions.

Rajendra has also been organising pani panchayat or water parliament in distant villages in Rajasthan to make people aware of the traditional water conservation wisdom, the urgency of ground water recharging for maintaining underground water table and advocating community control over natural resources. In 2005, he was awarded Jamnalal Bajaj award. In 2009, he led a padayatra (walkathon) a march of a group of environmentalists and NGOs through Mumbai city along the endangered Mithi river.

Clearly the contribution of Rajendra Singh in the field of water conservation and management is incredible.

16

Role of NGOs in Social Development

NGO stands for Non-Governmental Organisation. There is not any legally accepted universal definition of the respective term. In many jurisdictions NGOs are termed as non-profit organisations, private voluntary organisations, charities, third sector organisations and so on. The World Bank defines NGOs as "Private organisations that pursue activities to relieve sufferings, promote the interests of the poor, protect the environment, provide basic social services or undertake community development." An NGO is basically a legally constituted organisation which is operated by legal persons who act independently from any government. Generally NGO runs on the funds obtained from membership fees, donations and other charities. But in those cases where the NGOs are funded partially or completely by governments, the NGO restrained the government representatives from any membership in the organisation in order to sustain its 'non-governmental' status. NGO refers to the organisations that are excluded from any political and governmental framework and are not conventional as profit making businesses. Though NGOs pursue wider social aims that have political aspects, yet they are not openly political organisations such as political parties.

A World Bank key document, "Working with NGOs" adds, 'In wider usage, the term NGO can be applied to any non-profit organisation which is independent from government. NGOs are typically value based organisations which depend, in whole or in part, on charitable donations and voluntary services. Although the NGO sector has become increasingly professionalized over the last two decades, principles of voluntarism and altruism remain key defining characteristics'. The above mentioned document points out that 'since the mid 1970s, the NGO sector in both developed and developing countries has experienced exponential growth. It is now estimated that over 15 per cent of the total overseas development aid is channelized through NGOs'. That is roughly around USD 8 Billion!!!

There are approximately 40,000 NGOs operating internationally across the world. India has about 3.3 million NGOs; one NGO for every 400 people. Russia has about 277,000 NGOs, while USA has about 1.5 million NGOs.

Richard Robbins, professor of anthropology, in his book 'Global Problems and the Culture of Capitalism' (Allyn and Bacon, Second Edition, 2002, Page 128-129) suggests a few reasons why NGOs have become increasingly important in the past decades or so:

1. The end of the Cold War made it easier for NGOs to operate.

2. Communication advancements, especially the internet, have helped create new global communities and bonds between like-minded people across the state boundaries.

3. Increased resources, growing professionalism and more employment opportunities in NGOs.

4. The media's ability to inform more people about global problems leads to an increased awareness where the public may demand that their governments take action of some kind.

5. Perhaps the most important, Robbins suggests is that some believe NGOs have developed as a part of layer, neoliberal economic and political agenda. Shifts in economic and political ideology have lent to increasing support of NGOs from governments and official aid agencies in response.

The role and importance of NGOs in the social development of a country simply cannot be neglected. NGOs are non-state actors which play increasingly important roles in developing transitional and developed societies. Levels of international assistance received by the NGO sector have increased dramatically. The increasing resource flows, combined with the fact that NGOs receive a higher level of public exposure and scrutiny than ever before, speak to their continuing importance. Perhaps there is now a more realistic view among policy makers about what NGOs can and cannot achieve.

For Mitlin et al. (2005) the strength of development in NGOs remains in their potential role in constructing and demonstrating 'alternatives' to the status quo, which remains to be a need that has never been more pressing in the present scenario.

NGOs exist as alternatives. In being 'non-governmental' they constitute vehicles for people to participate in development and social change in ways that would not be possible through governmental programmes. In being 'non-governmental' they constitute a 'space' in which it is possible to think about development and social change in ways that would not be likely through government programmes... They constitute instruments for turning the alternative ideas and alternative forms of participation, into alternative practices and hard outcomes. The relationship of NGOs to development therefore takes many forms and their diversity cannot be overemphasized. For some, NGOs are useful actors because they can provide cost-effective services in flexible ways, while for others they are campaigners fighting for a change or generating new ideas and approaches to development problems.

NGOs bridge the gap between government services (which are meant for the welfare of the people) and the people and beneficiaries. Due to population growth, unavailability of proper delivery channels for these welfare services and corruption, the government is unable to cater to each and every citizen equally. In that case, NGOs are the solution to this issue. NGOs facilitate and catalyse the social participation of the people (which remain deprived of these welfare services) living in their respective countries and to bring a change towards betterment.

Hence, NGOs have their lions share in social development of a community, state and/or country.

17

Development in Different Indian Perspectives

Panchayati Raj: More than 70 per cent of the total population of India lives in rural India. It's quite clear that developed rural India means developed India i.e. in order to make India a developed nation; its rural areas must be catered with a prime focus of delivering better opportunities and services. Due to vast land area and huge population growth rate, Government of India, both at central and state level, cannot cater to each and every citizen of the country equally and in a harmonious way. This situation demands a decentralised channel of administration in rural India which can approach each and every person living in rural India i.e. villages. And this is why it gave rise to the establishment of a governance system termed as "Panchayati Raj" in India.

Panchayati Raj is a decentralized form of governance in which each village is responsible for its own affairs and in which gram panchayats are the basic units of administration. The word 'Panchayati Raj' is taken from Hindi language supported by Sanskrit etymology. '*Panch*' means five, '*ayat*' refers to a council or committee and '*raj*' means rule. Therefore, Panchayati Raj means rule of an elective council of five members organized in the republic of India as an organ of village self-government. Generally, a group of five influential older and wise men acknowledged by the community as its governing body is chosen or elected to constitute a Panchayat. The Sarpanch is the all in all and at the helm of the affairs in a Panchayat. Panchayati Raj is also considered as a South Asian political system which exists in Pakistan, Nepal and Bangladesh.

Panchayati Raj framework of governance comprises three levels of administration: Gram Panchayat (Village level), Janpad or Panchayat Samiti (Block level) and Zilla Parishad or Panchayat (District level).

On April 24, 1993 the Constitutional (73rd Amendment) Act 1992 came into force to provide with a constitutional status to the Panchayati Raj Institutions (PRIs). The union cabinet of the Government of India on August 27, 2009 approved 50% reservation for women in PRIs.

Panchayati Raj ensures greater participation of the people and more effective implementation of rural development programmes. The Constitutional (73rd Amendment) Act 1992 was meant to provide constitutional sanction to establish "democracy at the grassroots level as it is at the state level or national level." Its main features are as follows:

- The Gram Sabha or village assembly as a deliberative body to decentralised governance has been envisaged as the foundation of the Panchayati Raj System.

- A uniform three-tier structure of Panchayats at village (Gram Panchayat—GP), intermediate or block (Panchayat Samiti—PS) and district (Zilla Parishad—ZP) levels.

- All the seats in a panchayat at every level are to be filled by elections from respective territorial constituencies.

- Not less than one-third of the total seats for membership as well as office of chairpersons of each tier has to be reserved for women.

- Reservation for weaker castes and tribes (SCs and STs) has to be provided at all levels in proportion to their population in the panchayats.

- To supervise, direct and control the regular and smooth elections to panchayats, a State Election Commission has to be constituted in every State and UT.

- The Act has ensured constitution of a State Finance Commission in every State/UT, for every five years, to suggest measures to strengthen finances of panchayati raj institutions.

- To promote bottom-up-planning, the District Planning Committee (DPC) in every district has been accorded constitutional status.

- An indicative list of 29 items has been given in Eleventh Schedule of the Constitution. Panchayats are expected to play an effective role in planning and implementation of works related to these 29 items.

Ministry of Panchayati Raj, Government of India, states its vision as 'To attain decentralized and participatory local self-government through the Panchayati Raj Institutions'. It further states its mission as 'Empowerment, enablement and accountability of PRIs to ensure inclusive development with social justice and efficient delivery of services'.

Better and effective system of Panchayat administrations can facilitate the development process in rural India. People can speak their minds and can be heard by the panchayat on any conflicting issue. Panchayat can have a better administrative control and maximise its reach to the people. This will encourage people to participate in social matters related to their village; or matters related to them and ultimately with the cooperation of panchayat, their problems can be reported to higher levels of administration which will fasten the process of improvement and will bring a change; a change for the betterment of rural India. Hence strengthening of Panchayati Raj is the need of the hour in order to make India a developed nation.

Sanitation: Sanitation is the process of safe management and disposal of human excreta. The World Health Organisation states that: 'Sanitation generally refers to the provision of facilities and services for the safe disposal of human urine and faeces. Inadequate sanitation is a major cause of disease world-wide and improving sanitation is known to have a significant beneficial impact on health both in households and across communities. The word "sanitation" also refers to the maintenance of hygienic conditions, through services such as garbage collection and wastewater disposal.' Earlier the concept of sanitation was only limited to disposal of human excreta, but it also includes liquid and solid waste disposal, food, personal, domestic and environmental hygiene. Sanitation in simple terms refers to the prevention of human contact with the ill effects of wastes through hygienic means of promoting health. It also includes management and disposal of human wastes; waste water collection, treatment and reuse; and other onsite treatments.

The degree of sanitation cannot be measured in terms of physical outputs, that is by only measuring only i.e. by the number of toilets built, waste management services launched and/or kilometers of sewer system laid. Instead, the prime focus should be on maintaining these services smoothly for its efficient use. Dealing effectively with human waste may also require action in related areas such as water supply, drainage, and solid waste management. Good coordination between the agencies responsible for these services is, therefore, important.

Urban sanitation in India has many problems and hurdles viz. low infrastructural development, less service coverage, low service usage and weak institutional arrangements. Let us go through each of them in brief.

Low infrastructural development in the sanitation sector in urban India is one of the primary reasons of improper sanitation facilities in India. Though there have been development in sanitation infrastructure coverage in India yet it has failed so far to keep pace with the growing rate of urban population. If this will keep to be continued, it may take several years for sewerage and drainage services to properly reach to every human being in urban areas of India. Another factor hampering growth of sanitation facilities in India is the negligence of its need by a majority of the people as they probably don't appreciate the importance of sanitation.

Limited access to the sanitation services is another factor restricting the management and disposal of wastes. Sanitation facilities may be there for all the people in urban India but it could be unhygienic, inconvenient or unpleasant. This hinders the usage of these facilities by the people. In many areas there is no provision and arrangement for the treatment of these wastes. Lack of maintenance of these sanitation facilities again hampers the disposal of human excreta.

Low usage of the services provided by the sanitation facilities again gives a rise to the ill effects of improper sanitation. People are not aware of the use of the toilets and the facilities are unacceptable in some ways such as people may not be willing to share toilets. Such problems indicate the need for effective communication in sanitation programmes, so that community awareness, preferences and behavior are properly understood and then addressed through information, advice, and hygiene promotion.

Weak institutional arrangements in the field of sanitation such as lack of proper equipments and expertise, improper distribution of funds and investments meant for the development of sanitation sector, corruption, lack of awareness and unrealised responsibilities are also contributing in the degradation of sanitation facilities in India.

There are no specific legal provisions regarding to urban sanitation, but there are some provisions relating to sanitation services. Some of them are as follows:

74th Constitutional Amendment Act, 1992: It governs the responsibility for the planning and delivery of urban services, including sanitation. The 12th Schedule of the Act sets out a list of critical issues for the urban local bodies including, amongst other things: Urban planning; Regulation of land-use and construction of buildings; Water supply for domestic, industrial, and commercial purposes; Public health, sanitation, conservancy, and solid waste management; Protection of the environment and promotion of ecological aspects; and Slum improvement and upgrading.

The Environment (Protection) Act, 1986: This Act applies in principle to every establishment, agency, or individual discharging any pollutant into the environment. 'Pollutant' includes treated or untreated sewage. In principle, municipalities are required to comply with these discharge norms for effluent released from sewage treatment plants and to pay water cess under the Water Cess Act, 1977.

Apart from these provisions, some municipal bylaws also suggest and enable local bodies to discharge their functions in order to facilitate sanitation in their locality.

The Government of India has launched various schemes and missions in order to promote sanitation facilities in urban areas of the country. Some of them are as follows:

Integrated Low Cost Sanitation Scheme: The Government of India is implementing the Integrated Low Cost Sanitation Scheme since 1980. The Scheme, as revised with effect from January 2008, envisages conversion of dry latrines into low cost twin pit pour flush latrines and construction of new individual toilets to Economically Weaker Section (EWS) households who have no latrines in the urban areas of the country. Under the scheme the pattern of assistance is 75 per cent Central Subsidy, 15 per cent State Subsidy and 10 per cent beneficiary share. An Upper ceiling cost of Rs.15,000/- (Rs.10,000/- initially) is provided for the complete unit of a two pit pour flush individual latrine with superstructure (excluding states falling in difficult and hilly areas). For the States falling in the category of difficult and hilly areas, 25 per cent extra cost is provided for each two pit pour flush latrine. The Scheme is limited to Economically Weaker Section (EWS) households only and does not entail a loan component. The Scheme is implemented by Ministry of Housing & Urban Poverty Alleviation directly.

However, these schemes focuses on the provision of latrines/toilets and the elimination of open defecation and scavenging. It does not cover the problem of inadequate sanitation, including treatment and disposal of sewage and solid waste management, which has considerable environmental and health implications. The scope of urban sanitation is much larger than the issues covered under the Scheme for Integrated Low Cost Sanitation which essentially focuses on provision of latrines to prevent open defecation in order to eliminate manual scavenging.

The obnoxious practice of manual scavenging or engaging of fellow human beings into cleaning the untreated human excreta has been banned under the "Employment of Manual Scavengers and Construction of Dry Latrine (Prohibition) Act, 1993" which prohibits construction and/or maintenance of dry latrines and employment of manual scavengers.

The Cabinet Committee on Economic Affairs has approved the proposal of the Ministry of Housing and Urban Poverty Alleviation to extend the ongoing scheme of Integrated Low Cost Sanitation Scheme into the 12th Five Year Plan with revised features and cost estimates.

National Urban Sanitation Policy: The vision of the policy is that all 'Indian cities and towns become totally sanitised, healthy and livable and ensure and sustain good public health and environmental outcomes for all their citizens with a special focus on hygienic and affordable sanitation facilities for the urban poor and women.' The focus of the Policy is on Awareness Generation and Behavioural Change by generating awareness about sanitation and its linkages with public and environmental health amongst communities and institutions and also promoting mechanisms to bring about and sustain behavioural changes aimed at adoption of healthy sanitation practices.

Consumer Awareness: We start consuming since the moment we come to this world. We need oil, milk, clothes, services etc. in order to meet our requirements and needs. Thus, we all are consumers in the literal sense of the term. [A consumer is a buyer of goods and services. A person using the goods and services with the permission of the original buyer of products and/or services is also referred as a consumer. However, a person is not treated as a consumer if he/she purchases a product and/or service for resale purposes.]

The market is flooded with a large variety of goods and services to satisfy one's needs and requirements. When an individual purchases a product or service he/she expects the justified degree of durability, quality and quantity from that very product or service. But what to do if the goods and services bought are found out to be bad in quality or unreasonably priced or measured less in quantity etc. In such situations the consumers, instead of getting satisfaction, feel cheated by the sellers who have sold the goods and services. They also feel that they should be properly compensated for the loss. So there should be a system to redress such issues. On the other hand consumers should also realize that they do have responsibilities not just rights. This gives rise to "consumer awareness" i.e. the accumulation of the state where consumers are aware of what (products, services etc.) is purchased or bought by them.

A consumer is not aware until and unless he/she does possess the knowledge of the quality of the product/service purchased by him/her; the education about different types of hazards and problems associated with the marketing of the product or service (advertisements); the consumer rights and knowledge about his/her own responsibilities as a consumer.

Consumers are the basic functional unit for facilitation of the economy of the state. They contribute a lot in improving the standard of living as they own and afford different types of products and services to upgrade their lives. This ultimately adds up to the Human Development Index (HDI) of the country pushing it towards a change for betterment i.e. development.

To safeguard the interests of the consumers in India, Government of India has legal and administrative provisions in the field of consumer education in our country. The major consumer redressal systems (It comprises of the Laws to protect the interest of the consumers and the Institutions to enforce the laws to uphold consumers' rights.) are as follows:

Consumer Protection Act, 1986: This is an act from the Parliament of India which makes a provision for the establishment of consumer councils and other authorities for the settlement of consumers' disputes and for matters connected therewith.

The National Consumer Disputes Redressal Commission (NCDRC) states the following about this Act: 'The Consumer Protection Act, 1986 (in short, 'the Act'), is a benevolent social legislation that lays down the rights of the consumers and provides there for promotion and protection of the rights of the consumers. The first and the only Act of its kind in India, it has enabled ordinary consumers to secure less expensive and often speedy redressal of their grievances. By spelling out the rights and remedies of the consumers in a market so far dominated by organised manufacturers and traders of goods and providers of various types of services, the Act makes the dictum, caveat emptor ('buyer beware') a thing of the past.

The Act mandates establishment of Consumer Protection Councils at the Centre as well as in each State and District, with a view to promoting consumer awareness.

To provide inexpensive, speedy and summary redressal of consumer disputes, quasi-judicial bodies have been set up in each District and State and at the National level, called the District Forums, the State Consumer Disputes Redressal Commissions and the National Consumer Disputes Redressal Commission respectively. At present, there are 629 District Forums and 35 State Commissions with the National Consumer

Disputes Redressal Commission (NCDRC) at its apex. NCDRC has its office at Upbhokta Naya Bhawan, 'F' Block, GPO Complex, INA, New Delhi-110 023.

The provisions of this Act covers 'goods' as well as 'services'. The goods are those which are manufactured or produced and sold to consumers through wholesalers and retailers. The services are in the nature of transport, telephone, electricity, housing, banking, insurance, medical treatment, etc.

If a consumer is not satisfied by the decision of a District Forum, he can appeal to the State Commission. Against the order of the State Commission a consumer can come to the National Commission."

The CPA was enacted to provide cheap, simple and quick justice to the millions of consumers in the country. CPA ensures a justice which is less formal, involves less paperwork, cut delays and is less expensive. This Act applies to all goods and services, unless specifically exempted. For non-compliance of the order of the District Forum, State Commission or National Commission, the person concerned shall be punishable with imprisonment of not less than one month which may extend to three years or with fine which shall not be less than Rs. 2000 but extend up to Rs. 10,000 or with both.

Prevention of Food Adulteration Act, 1954: Food is an essential element in order to sustain in life. Nutritious, healthy, fresh and pure diet is the most essential for the health of the people. In fact it would not be wrong to say that an individual's health ultimately adds up to nation's wealth. Adulteration of food articles was a very persistent anti-social factor in initial years after the independence of the country. To prevent this, Government of India realised a need for a regulation which safeguards the maintenance of the standard and quality of the food items in India.

As a result of this, The Prevention of Food Adulteration Bill was passed by both the house of Parliament and received the assent of the President on 29 September, 1954. It came into force on 1 June, 1955 as The Prevention of Food Adulteration Act, 1954 (37 of 1954).

Food Safety and Standards Authority of India states that 'The Act was promulgated by Parliament in 1954 to make provision for the prevention of adulteration of food, along with the Prevention of Food Adulteration Rules, 1955 which was incorporated in 1955 as an extension to the Act. Broadly, the PFA Act covers food standards, general procedures for sampling, analysis of food, powers of authorized officers, nature of penalties and other parameters related to food. It deals with parameters relating to food additives, preservative, coloring matters, packing and labeling of foods, prohibition and regulations of sales etc.'

According to this Act, guilt will be punished with imprisonment for a term which shall not be less than six months and up to 3 years and with fine up to one thousand rupees.

Essential Commodities Act, 1955: This Act is intended to provide, in the interest of the general public, for the control of the production, supply and distribution of, and trade and commerce, in certain commodities. This act ensures the accumulation and delivery of certain products or goods which are essential (according to Government) for living a life with decent standards. According to the Government, the scarcity or obstruction in delivery of these 'essential' products due to hoarding or black-marketing could affect the normal life of the people in a major way.

The mentioned 'essential' commodities under this Act are cattle fodder including oilcakes and other concentrates, coal and other derivatives, component parts and accessories of automobiles, cotton and woollen textiles, drugs, foodstuffs, iron and steel, paper, petroleum products, raw jute, raw cotton and cotton seed. The Act gives power to control production, supply, distribution etc. of commodities for maintaining or increasing supplies and for securing their equitable distribution and availability at fair prices.

The Standard of Weights and Measures Act, 1976: This is another piece of Indian legislation for consumer welfare. This Act is intended to introduce a standard in relation to weight and measures used in trade and commerce. The main aim is to sub-serve the interests of the consumers.

The Act serves to the following purposes like replacement of the bewildering varieties of weights and measurements in use in the country by standards based on metric system and provide better protection to consumers by ensuring accuracy in weights and measures.

The Act enlists the objectives like establishment of standards of weight and measures; regulation of interstate trade and commerce in weights and measures and other goods which are sold or distributed by weight, number and measurement.

There is a provision of penalty under this Act viz. a fine of Rs. 500/- to Rs. 1000/- and imprisonment up to seven years, if violation (use of non-metric system for weights and measures) of any provision of the Act is found. Respective authorities also have the power to inspect, search, seize and forfeit the goods involved in the offence.

Wildlife and Forest Conservation: Wildlife conservation is the practice of protecting those plants and animal species which are on the brink of extinction along with their natural habitat. One of the ethical goals of wildlife conservation is to ensure the existence of wilderness and wildlife so that our future generations can enjoy and recognize its importance. Earth is the only known living planet because of its special environment and ecological conditions that are life supporting. Forest and wildlife are an integral part of our life. Forest and their by-products and wildlife contribute in our day=today life, directly or indirectly. Forest and wildlife are one of the most important and valuable resources that are gifted to us by the nature.

Some of the major threats to the wildlife can be categorised as habitat loss, climatic change, use of pesticides and toxic chemicals, unregulated poaching and hunting, natural phenomena (floods, earthquakes, volcanoes, lightning and forest fires), pollution, over exploitation of resources, extremely growing indifference of the public to the wildlife, conservation and environment in general.

The importance of the forest and wildlife should be valued and recognized by both government and nongovernmental sectors. Even an individual must respect the gifts of forest and wildlife. Forests supply timber, fuel, medicines, wood and raw materials for many industries. Apart from these products, forests play a key role in the maintenance of climate, rain patterns, water and soil conservation. Forests also act as home for various tribal civilisations across the globe.

Due to mindless destruction of forest and wildlife, there is an urgent need for regulating this anti-social practice. Apart from the governments in many countries of the world, NGOs are contributing a lot in the field of wildlife and forest conservation. The main NGOs in this field are WWF (World Wide Fund for Nature; earlier known as World Wildlife Fund. It is the world's largest independent conservation organization with over 5 million supporters worldwide working in more than 90 countries.); The Nature Conservancy (US charitable environment organization); Wildlife Conservation Society, Audubon Society; Safari Club International and Wild Earth Guardians etc.

Now let us discuss wildlife and forest conservation with Indian perspective.

Wildlife in India is very rich and diverse in its parameter. Apart from some major domestic and farm animals such as cows, buffaloes, goats, sheep and poultry India has a wide variety of animals such as tiger, loin, wild leopard, pythons, foxes, bears, wolves, rhino, crocodiles, camels, wild dogs, Asian elephants, deer species, monkeys, snakes, antelope species and bison.

India lying with the Indomalayan ecozone (extends across most of south and southeast Asia and into sudden parts of east Asia) is a home to about 7.6 per cent of all mammalian, 12.6 per cent of avian, 6.2 per cent of reptilian and 6.0 per cent of flowering plants species.

Like all other nations, India too is encountering with the destruction of forest and depletion of wildlife. This anti-social practice has been a matter of serious concern since last four decades in India. The growing greed of human to over exploit the resources provided by the forests, the illegal trade of the animals' skins, tusks, ivory etc. is adding fuel to the process of destruction of the forests and wildlife. India has about 20 per cent of the world's population with only 2.5 per cent of the total land area of the world. This compels the people to clear out the forested land in order to create space for their living. Contractors and builders are making housing complexes and industries in forest area of India as there is no space left in the cities for further development. This again is posing a serious threat to wildlife and forest conservation. Apart from this overgrazing is also taking its own toll.

To check these types of activities and to protect wildlife and forests in India, the government launched *The Wildlife Protection Act, 1972.*

It is a legislation enacted by the Parliament of India on 9th September, 1972 for protection of plant and animal species. In official language, the definition of the Act states it as 'An Act to provide for the protection of wild animals and birds and for matters connected therewith or any ancillary or incident thereto'. However this Act extends to the whole of India except the state of Jammu and Kashmir as it has its own environment Act.

Another scheme *'Project Tiger'* has also played a vital role in protection of the tigers in India. This project was started by Padma Shri Kailash Sankhala, who was a renowned naturalist and conservationist of India. Kailash Sankhala was popularly known as the Tiger Man of the India across the globe. This project is the world's largest wildlife conservations programme set up in India in 1973. 'The main objective of Project Tiger is to ensure a viable population of tigers in India for scientific, economic, aesthetic, cultural and ecological values and to preserve for all time, areas of biological importance as natural heritage for the benefit to education and enjoyment of the people. This scheme includes wildlife management, protection measures, site specific ecodevelopment to reduce the dependency of local communities on tiger reserve resources.'

Apart from this project, another social campaign named, *'Save Our Tigers'* was launched by NDTV and Aircel with an aim to create awareness about the alarming state of the tiger in the country at the moment, encourage tiger conservation and save tigers from extinction.

Indian forests need to be managed as forestry is the second largest land use in India after agriculture, covering about 641,130 sq. km or 22 per cent of the total geographical area of the country. When it comes to conservation of forests and wildlife in India, one simply cannot neglect the legacy of *Joint Forest Management (JFM)*.

Initially JFM was originated in 1971 at Arabari Forest Range in Midnapore town in West Bengal. JFM is the most efficient way of forest management in India as it is more approaching initiative. It is a collaborative management regime, initiated by the Ministry of Environment of Forest, Government of India in the 1990s (full implementation) building a partnership with the local communities for rehabilitation of the degraded forests. It is basically the arrangement for the partnership in forest management involving both the state forest departments and local communities living close to forests. Local people are informed, persuaded and are made aware of the importance of the forests. This motivates them to take a step forward in protecting the forest and wildlife of their respective region. As a result of this, villagers agree to assist the state forest department in the safeguarding of forest resources from fire, over grazing and illegal harvesting.

The local forest committee is also known as Forest Protection Committee (FPC) receives non timber forest products and a share of the revenue from the sale of timber products in exchange of their assistance to the government in protecting forests.

JnNURM: Have you ever noticed any of the Delhi Transport Corporation's (DTC) Green Low Floor Buses? If yes, then have you seen 'JnNURM' written on the bus? If yes, then ever wondered what does it means; ever tried to find out? Well I guess the answer is NO. So let us discuss about JnNURM.

JnNURM stands for Jawaharlal Nehru National Urban Renewal Mission. It is actually a broad scale city development and modernisation scheme launched by the Government of India under Ministry of Urban Development. This scheme was officially inaugurated by prime minister Manmohan Singh on December 3, 2005. This scheme was intended to bring a change in the quality of life and infrastructure in the cities of India. Various sub schemes were also launched under this massive initiative in order to bring improvement in the civic services of the cities.

The mission statement of JnNURM as stated on their official website is, 'The aim is to encourage reforms and fast track planned development of identified cities. Focus is to be on efficiency in urban infrastructure and service delivery mechanisms, community participation, and accountability of ULBs (Urban Local Bodies)/ Parastatal agencies towards citizens.'

The objectives of the JnNURM are to ensure that the following are achieved in the urban sector:

(a) Focused attention to integrated development of infrastructure services in cities covered under the Mission;

(b) Establishment of linkages between asset-creation and asset-management through a slew of reforms for long-term project sustainability;

(c) Ensuring adequate funds to meet the deficiencies in urban infrastructural services;

(d) Planned development of identified cities including peri-urban areas, outgrowths and urban corridors leading to dispersed urbanisation;

(e) Scale-up delivery of civic amenities and provision of utilities with emphasis on universal access to the urban poor;

(f) Special focus on urban renewal programme for the old city areas to reduce congestion; and

(g) Provision of basic services to the urban poor including security of tenure at affordable prices, improved housing, water supply and sanitation, and ensuring delivery of other existing universal services of the government for education, health and social security.

Though the name is Urban Renewable Mission, yet this scheme focuses on the development of rural areas, especially underdeveloped rural sectors across the country. It is a mega project launched by the Government of India which sets up a whole new avenue for development programmes running in the country.

And lastly, It's not only Delhi's DTC low floor buses which have been started under this scheme. Low floor buses in Thiruvananthapuram, Coimbatore and Kolkata (West Bengal Transport Infrastructure Development Corporation Limited) are also started under the same scheme.

References for Additional Information

"50 People Who Could Save The Planet"; The Guardian, January 5, 2008.

A Comprehensive Theory of Social Development by Garry Jacobs, Robert Macfarlane, N. Asokan; International Centre for Peace and Development, Napa, California, USA.

AOEMA, 2005; UN Department of Economic and Social Affairs; UN e Government Survey 2012.

Biography of Rajendra Singh; Magsaysay Award Website, 2001.

"Communication for Development and Social Change", ISBN: 978-81-7829-772-9, Sage Publications.

Center of Digital Government. "ENGAGE: Creating e government that supports commerce, collaboration, community and common wealth": 2008. www.nicusa.com.

Clift, Steven, "E Democracy, E Governance and Public Net-Work" www.publicus.net, September 2003; http://www.publicus.net/articles/edempublicnetwork.html.

"Encyclopaedia of Governance." By Mark Bevir, Sage Publications. Publication Year: 2007, Online Publication Date: September 15, 2007, DOI: 10.4135/9781412952613, Print ISBN: 9781412905794, Online ISBN: 9781412952613.

"First Official Estimate: An NGO for Every 400 People in India"; The Indian Express. July 7, 2010.

"Hobbled NGOs Wary of Medvedev"; Chicago Tribune. May 7, 2008.

Indira Gandhi Conservation Monitoring Centre (IGCMC), New Delhi; The United Nations Environmental Programme (UNEP), World Conservation Monitoring Centre, Cambridge, UK, 2001.

ITC: e choupal: Let's Put India First; itcportal.com.

"India: More NGOs, Than Schools and Health Centers"; oneworld.net; July 7, 2010.

Jeong Chun Hai, 2007; Fundamental of Development Administration: Scholar Press. ISBN: 978-967-5-045080.

Module 1, Page No. 8, Development Communication Sourcebook, World Bank. ISBN: 978-0-8213-7522-8, ISBN: 978-0-8213-7523-5.

Mody Beller (1991) Designing Messages for Development Communication, New Delhi, Sage Publication.

National Commission to review the working of The Constitution. A Consultation Paper on Literacy in the context of The Constitution of India. (September 26, 2001, Vigyan Bhawan Annexe, New Delhi - 110011).http://lawmin.nic.in/ncrwc/finalreport/v2b1-5.htm.

National open university of Nigeria, Page No. 9, ISBN: 978-058-251-7.

Nora Cruz Quebral, "Development Communication Primer", ISBN: 978-983-9054-56-9, Southbound Penang.

"Non-Governmental Organizations and Development"; David Lewis and Nazneen Kanji, 2009; Routledge (Taylor & Francis Group). ISBN: 978-0-415-45429-2 (hbk), ISBN: 978-0-415-45430-8 (pbk), ISBN: 978-0-203-87707-4 (ebk).

Official website of SEWA, http://www.sewa.org/.

Press Information Bureau, Release ID: 62600; Release ID: 89273.

Quebral, Nora (23 November 2001). "Development Communication in a Borderless World". Paper presented at the national conference-workshop on the undergraduate development communication curriculum, "New Dimensions, Bold Decisions". Continuing Education Centre, UP Los Baños: Department of Science Communication, College of Development Communication, University of the Philippines Los Baños. pp. 15–28.

S. Ganesh (1994) Lectures on Mass Communication, New Delhi, Indian Publishers.

Social Watch Archives, http://www.socialwatch.org/node/15915.

TM Thomas Issac with Richard Franke: Local Democracy and Development - Peoples' Campaign for Decentralized Planning in Kerala; New Delhi, Leftword Books, p. 19. (2000).

"Waterman of India plans a river parliament to revive the Mithi"; Indian Express, January 12, 2009.

http://oxforddictionaries.com/definition/english/development.

http://www.volunteeringoptions.org/VolunteeringDevelopment/
WhatisDevelopment/tabid/78/Default.aspx.

http://en.wikipedia.org/wiki/Development.

http://archive.lib.msu.edu/DMC/African%20Journals/pdfs/
africa%20media%20review/vol3no3/jamr003003002.pdf.

http://www.icpd.org/development_theory/comprehensive_
theory_of_social_development.htm#ProcessofEmergence.

http://en.wikipedia.org/wiki/Development_communication.

http://share.pdfonline.com/359bfdd0cf8e4e848fd29330a5991c21/
LECTURE%20ON%20DEVELOPMENT%20COMMUNICATION
%20LESSON%201(3)%20(1).htm.

http://www.cdcepp.org/the-conference/.

http://go.worldbank.org/5CHGCEWM70.

http://archive.lib.msu.edu/DMC/African%20Journals/pdfs/
africa%20media%20review/vol3no3/jamr003003002.pdf; Page No. 5,
Africa Media Review.Vol. 3 No. 3, 1989 (perspective on development
communication).

http://www.happyplanetindex.org/.

http://www.unmillenniumproject.org/goals/.

http://www.thehindu.com/opinion/lead/millennium-development-goals-india/
article838318.ece.

http://articles.economictimes.indiatimes.com/2013-01-01/news/
36094108_1_mdgs-child-mortality-poverty-ratio.

http://zeenews.india.com/business/news/economy/india-will-not-be-able-to-
achieve-crucial-mdg-targets-report_67303.html.

http://indianmedicine.nic.in/index2.asp?slid=19&sublinkid= 15&lang=1
department of AYUSH.

http://www.humanrights.gov/2012/01/12/fact-sheet-non-governmental-
organizations-ngos-in-the-united-states/.

http://www.projecttiger.nic.in.

http://jnnurm.nic.in/wp-content/uploads/2011/01/Prime-Ministers-
Office.htm.

Index